Lake Oswego Jr. High
2500 SW Country Club Rd.
Lake Oswego, OR 97034
503-534-2335

# Causes of the Civil War:
## The Differences Between the North and South

THE CIVIL WAR
A NATION DIVIDED

THE
# CIVIL WAR
## A NATION DIVIDED

# Causes of the Civil War:
## The Differences Between the North and South

**Shane Mountjoy, Ph.D.** / Consulting Editor **Tim McNeese**

**CHELSEA HOUSE**
PUBLISHERS
An imprint of Infobase Publishing

**CAUSES OF THE CIVIL WAR:**
**THE DIFFERENCES BETWEEN THE NORTH AND SOUTH**

Chelsea House
An imprint of Infobase Publishing
132 West 31st Street
New York, NY 10001

**Library of Congress Cataloging-in-Publication Data**
Mountjoy, Shane, 1967–
  Causes of the Civil War : the differences between the North and South / by Shane Mountjoy.
      p. cm. — (The Civil War : a nation divided)
  Includes bibliographical references and index.
  ISBN 978-1-60413-036-2 (hardcover)
  1. United States—History—Civil War, 1861–1865—Causes—Juvenile literature.
  2. United States—Politics and government—1849–1861—Juvenile literature.
  I. Title. II. Series.

  E459.M93 2009
  973.7'11—dc22              2008030242

Chelsea House books are available at special discounts when purchased in bulk quantities for businesses, associations, institutions, or sales promotions. Please call our Special Sales Department in New York at (212) 967-8800 or (800) 322-8755.

You can find Chelsea House on the World Wide Web at
http://www.chelseahouse.com

Series design by Lina Farinella
Cover design by Takeshi Takahashi and Keith Trego
Composition by North Market Street Graphics
Cover printed by Bang Printing, Brainerd, MN
Book printed and bound by Bang Printing, Brainerd, MN
Date printed: March, 2010

Printed in the United States of America

10 9 8 7 6 5 4 3 2

This book is printed on acid-free paper.

All links and Web addresses were checked and verified to be correct at the time of publication. Because of the dynamic nature of the Web, some addresses and links may have changed since publication and may no longer be valid.

# Contents

# Chronology

1820  The Missouri Compromise allows Maine to be admitted to the Union as a free state and Missouri as a slave state in 1821.

1831  William Lloyd Garrison publishes the first issue of his abolitionist newspaper, *The Liberator*.

1836  The House of Representatives passes a gag rule that automatically tables or postpones action on all petitions relating to slavery without hearing them.

1838  The Underground Railroad is formally organized.

1845  Former slave Frederick Douglass publishes his autobiography, *Narrative of the Life of Frederick Douglass, An American Slave*.

1850  Congress enacts several measures that together make up the Compromise of 1850.

1852  Harriet Beecher Stowe publishes *Uncle Tom's Cabin*.

1854  Congress passes the Kansas-Nebraska Act, which overturns the Missouri Compromise and thus opens northern territories to slavery.

1855  As Kansas prepares to vote, thousands of Border Ruffians from Missouri enter the territory in an attempt to influence the elections. This begins the period known as Bleeding Kansas.

1856  South Carolina representative Preston Brooks attacks Massachusetts senator Charles Sumner on the Senate floor and beats him with a cane.

**1857**     The Supreme Court rules, in *Dred Scott v. Sandford,* that blacks are not U.S. citizens and slaveholders have the right to take slaves into free areas of the country.

**1859**     John Brown seizes the arsenal at Harpers Ferry, Virginia. Robert E. Lee, then a Federal Army regular, leads the troops that capture Brown.

**1860**     **NOVEMBER**   Abraham Lincoln is elected president.

**DECEMBER**   A South Carolina convention passes an ordinance of secession, and the state secedes from the Union.

**1861**     **JANUARY**   Florida, Alabama, Georgia, and Louisiana secede from the Union.

**FEBRUARY**   Texas votes to secede from the Union. The Confederate States of America is formed and elects Jefferson Davis as its president.

**MARCH**   Abraham Lincoln is sworn in as the sixteenth president of the United States and delivers his first inaugural address.

**APRIL 12**   At 4:30 A.M., Confederate forces fire on South Carolina's Fort Sumter. The Civil War begins. Virginia secedes from the Union five days later.

**MAY**   Arkansas and North Carolina secede from the Union.

**JUNE**   Tennessee secedes from the Union.

**JULY 21**   The Union suffers a defeat in northern Virginia, at the First Battle of Bull Run (Manassas).

**AUGUST**   The Confederates win the Battle of Wilson's Creek, in Missouri.

**1862**     **FEBRUARY 6**   In Tennessee, Union general Ulysses S. Grant captures Fort Henry. Ten days later, he captures Fort Donelson.

**MARCH** The Confederate ironclad ship CSS *Virginia* (formerly the USS *Merrimack*) battles the Union ironclad *Monitor* to a draw. The Union's Peninsular Campaign begins in Virginia.

**APRIL 6–7** Ulysses S. Grant defeats Confederate forces in the Battle of Shiloh (Pittsburg Landing), in Tennessee.

**APRIL 24** David Farragut moves his fleet of Union navy vessels up the Mississippi River to take New Orleans.

**MAY 31** The Battle of Seven Pines (Fair Oaks) takes place in Virginia.

**JUNE 1** Robert E. Lee assumes command of the Army of Northern Virginia.

**JUNE 25–JULY 1** The Seven Days Battles are fought in Virginia.

**AUGUST 29–30** The Union is defeated at the Second Battle of Bull Run.

**SEPTEMBER 17** The bloodiest day in U.S. military history: Confederate forces under Robert E. Lee are stopped at Antietam, Maryland, by Union forces under George B. McClellan.

**SEPTEMBER 22** The first Emancipation Proclamation to free slaves in the rebellious states is issued by President Lincoln.

**DECEMBER 13** The Union's Army of the Potomac, under Ambrose Burnside, suffers a costly defeat at Fredericksburg, Virginia.

**1863**    **JANUARY 1** President Lincoln issues the final Emancipation Proclamation.

**JANUARY 29** Ulysses S. Grant is placed in command of the Army of the West, with orders to capture Vicksburg, Mississippi.

**MAY 1–4**  Union forces under Joseph Hooker are defeated decisively by Robert E. Lee's much smaller forces at the Battle of Chancellorsville, in Virginia.

**MAY 10**  The South suffers a huge blow as General Thomas "Stonewall" Jackson dies from wounds he received during the battle of Chancellorsville.

**JUNE 3**  Robert E. Lee launches his second invasion of the North; he heads into Pennsylvania with 75,000 Confederate troops.

**JULY 1–3**  The tide of war turns against the South as the Confederates are defeated at the Battle of Gettysburg in Pennsylvania.

**JULY 4**  Vicksburg, the last Confederate stronghold on the Mississippi River, surrenders to Ulysses S. Grant after a six-week siege.

**JULY 13–16**  Antidraft riots rip through New York City.

**JULY 18**  The black 54th Massachusetts Infantry Regiment under Colonel Robert Gould Shaw assaults a fortified Confederate position at Fort Wagner, South Carolina.

**SEPTEMBER 19–20**  A decisive Confederate victory takes place at Chickamauga, Tennessee.

**NOVEMBER 19**  President Lincoln delivers the Gettysburg Address.

**NOVEMBER 23–25**  Ulysses S. Grant's Union forces win an important victory at the Battle of Chattanooga, in Tennessee.

1864  **MARCH 9**  President Lincoln names Ulysses S. Grant general-in-chief of all the armies of the United States.

**MAY 4**  Ulysses S. Grant opens a massive, coordinated campaign against Robert E. Lee's Confederate armies in Virginia.

**MAY 5–6**  The Battle of the Wilderness is fought in Virginia.

**MAY 8–12**   The Battle of Spotsylvania is fought in Virginia.

**JUNE 1–3**   The Battle of Cold Harbor is fought in Virginia.

**JUNE 15**   Union forces miss an opportunity to capture Petersburg, Virginia; this results in a nine-month Union siege of the city.

**SEPTEMBER 2**   Atlanta, Georgia, is captured by Union forces led by William Tecumseh Sherman.

**OCTOBER 19**   Union general Philip H. Sheridan wins a decisive victory over Confederate general Jubal Early in the Shenandoah Valley of Virginia.

**NOVEMBER 8**   Abraham Lincoln is reelected president, defeating Democratic challenger George B. McClellan.

**NOVEMBER 15**   General William T. Sherman begins his March to the Sea from Atlanta.

**DECEMBER 15–16**   Confederate general John Bell Hood is defeated at Nashville, Tennessee, by Union forces under George H. Thomas.

**DECEMBER 21**   General Sherman reaches Savannah, Georgia; he leaves behind a path of destruction 300 miles long and 60 miles wide from Atlanta to the sea.

**1865**   Southern states begin to pass Black Codes.

**JANUARY 31**   The U.S. Congress approves the Thirteenth Amendment to the United States Constitution.

**FEBRUARY 3**   A peace conference takes place as President Lincoln meets with Confederate Vice President Alexander Stephens at Hampton Roads, Virginia; the meeting ends in failure, and the war continues.

**MARCH 4**   Lincoln delivers his second inaugural address ("With Malice Toward None"). Congress establishes the Freedmen's Bureau.

**MARCH 25**   Robert E. Lee's Army of Northern Virginia begins its last offensive with an attack on the center of

Ulysses S. Grant's forces at Petersburg, Virginia. Four hours later, Lee's attack is broken.

**APRIL 2**   Grant's forces begin a general advance and break through Lee's lines at Petersburg. Lee evacuates Petersburg. Richmond, Virginia, the Confederate capital, is evacuated.

**APRIL 9**   Robert E. Lee surrenders his Confederate Army to Ulysses S. Grant at the village of Appomattox Court House, Virginia.

**APRIL 14**   John Wilkes Booth shoots President Lincoln at Ford's Theatre in Washington, D.C.

**APRIL 15**   President Abraham Lincoln dies. Vice President Andrew Johnson assumes the presidency.

**APRIL 18**   Confederate general Joseph E. Johnston surrenders to Union general William T. Sherman in North Carolina.

**APRIL 26**   John Wilkes Booth is shot and killed in a tobacco barn in Virginia.

**DECEMBER**   The Thirteenth Amendment is ratified.

**1866**   Congress approves the Fourteenth Amendment to the Constitution.

Congress passes the Civil Rights Act.

The responsibilities and powers of the Freedmen's Bureau are expanded by Congress. The legislation is vetoed by President Johnson, but Congress overrides his veto.

The Ku Klux Klan is established in Tennessee.

**1867**   Congress passes the Military Reconstruction Act.

Congress passes the Tenure of Office Act.

**1868**   The impeachment trial of President Andrew Johnson ends in acquittal.

Ulysses S. Grant is elected president.

1869    Congress approves the Fifteenth Amendment to the Constitution.

1871    The Ku Klux Klan Act is passed by Congress.

1872    President Grant is reelected.

1875    A new Civil Rights Act is passed.

1877    Rutherford B. Hayes assumes the presidency.

The Reconstruction Era ends.

# One Nation, Two Sections

It is often difficult, if not impossible, to determine exactly what caused many great conflicts. The U.S. Civil War is no different. Indeed, the simple answer is slavery. It is true that slavery was the key difference between the North and the South during the early nineteenth century. But there were many other differences between the two regions. Some of the differences date back to the colonial period, when each colony was founded for different reasons.

These differences continued to develop throughout the nineteenth century until 1861 when a bloody civil war broke out in the United States between the North and the South. The conflict was the result of several decades of tension between the two sides. Americans had formed the United States with the ratification of the Constitution in 1788 and several states joined the Union after the original 13 states formed their new nation. The growing nation, however, faced the serious threat of falling apart from the very beginning. Each state had its own interests. Each state felt some commitment to its region. In time, the differences between the two sections grew more pronounced. But the most obvious difference between North and South remained the same—slavery.

## TWO AMERICAN SOCIETIES

The United States experienced rapid territorial expansion throughout the first half of the nineteenth century, beginning with the Louisiana Purchase in 1803 and ending with the Mexican-American War (1846–1848). During that half-century, the young republic progressed from a small collection of former British colonies on the eastern seaboard of North America to a nation stretching across a continent. In many ways, however, the United States was more a loose collection of states than a unified nation.

As Americans extended their control over the continent, they began to build more national unity. To do this, the national government began to exercise more power than the states did over economic issues and other matters. Not all Americans wanted to see more power in the hands of the national government. The supporters of each ideal were mostly clustered in different sections of the country. Thus, the disagreement over the role of the national government became intense as each section struggled for power to influence the direction of the nation.

Sectionalism did not suddenly appear in the 1840s and 1850s. Rather, the roots of sectionalism trace back to the colonial period. The New England colonies (Massachusetts, Rhode Island, Connecticut, and New Hampshire) differed from the mid-Atlantic colonies (New York, New Jersey, Pennsylvania, and Delaware). Both of these groups also differed from colonies in the South (Georgia, South Carolina, North Carolina, Virginia, and Maryland). These differences included things such as approaches to religion, basis for economic stability, and the role of slavery. Sectional differences were not new after 1800; what was new was the power of sectional differences to change the political landscape.

Increased passion and intensity about certain issues reflect the ways in which sectionalism changed after the Revolutionary War. Economically, there were four well-defined sections of the country: the Northeast, Southeast, Northwest, and Southwest. The economy of the Northeast (New England) was built upon industrial manufacturing, commercial trade, and large cities. The Southeast, made up of the original Southern states, relied upon the plantation system, and in the 1800s its economic prosperity was declining. The agricultural region of the Northwest (Ohio, Indiana, Illinois, Michigan, and Wisconsin) was growing at a fast pace as settlers pushed into fertile and unplowed lands to establish farms. Federal policy continued to push Native Americans westward, opening up the lands for settlers from the East and immigrants from Europe. The growth of canals and railroads allowed settlers in the Northwest to ship their goods to markets in the East. Finally, the cash crop of cotton fueled the growth of the Southwest (Tennessee, Mississippi, Arkansas, Louisiana, and Texas). Each of these sections stood somewhat independent of the others. As the nation grew, however, the four regions increasingly began to consider themselves as two sections: North and South. The clearest characteristic that separated them was slavery.

Slavery had traditionally been confined mostly to the Southeast, but an economic boom in cotton led to the expansion of slavery into the Southwest. Thus, just when it appeared slavery was fading, the institution suddenly found new life as the United States extended its western borders. Slavery helped tie the two Southern sections together, resulting in a unified South in 1860, on the eve of the Civil War.

Slavery was not the only issue that defined the two regions, however. Other characteristics also separated the North and the South. The North continued to grow in population, in large part due to European immigration. The rise of manufacturing in the North helped attract millions of immigrants to the country.

The Northeast and the Northwest were linked economically. In the 1830s, man-made canals helped encourage economic activity and transportation between the Northeast and Northwest.

By 1840, many began turning to railroads to transport raw materials, manufactured goods, and passengers. Western farmers shipped their agricultural goods back East. The same trains carried products made in Northern factories to customers in the West. Soon, the Northwest and the Northeast shared economic relationships that linked the two sections to each other. With the two regions of the North connected economically, it was not long before both grew closer socially and politically as well.

In addition to its advantages in industry and population, the North also held an advantage over the South in transportation. In 1840, the United States had 2,818 miles (4,535 kilometers) of working railroad track. A decade later, the mileage had risen to 9,021 (14,518 km). During the 1850s, the amount of mileage more than tripled. Most of the growth occurred in the North, especially the Northeast. In contrast, the South was the region that experienced the least amount of railroad growth during the 1850s. In 1861, Confederate states had less than half as many miles of railroad tracks as did Northern states.

Similarly, the use of the telegraph rose rapidly in the years just prior to the war. By 1860, the United States had strung more than 50,000 miles (80,500 km) of telegraph wire, linking cities all across the country. By the time war broke out in 1861, a telegraph line connected New York with San Francisco—the world's first transcontinental telegraph. (The impact of the transcontinental line was immediately clear when the celebrated Pony Express shut down just two days later.) Telegraph lines usually paralleled railroad tracks, linking cities and businesses throughout the North. Although both sections of the country had access to telegraph services, the North enjoyed more miles of telegraph lines than did the South.

It is true that there were many differences between the two regions. Yet, the main difference between the North and South

*The polarizing issue of slavery divided the United States into two distinct regions: the North and the South. People in the industrialized North did not use slave labor; the South, however, relied on slaves to produce cotton crops, which made up 57 percent of U.S. exports in 1860. Slavery, along with other issues regarding states' rights and dispute over new territories, was one of the main causes of the Civil War.*

was slavery. Moreover, the slavery issue drew out the most intense emotions and hostility between the two sections. What, then, caused the war?

## POSSIBLE CAUSES OF THE WAR

Slavery lay at the root of much of the hostility between the two sections of the young nation. On June 16, 1858, the Illinois Republican Party chose Abraham Lincoln as its nominee for the U.S. Senate seat, running against incumbent Stephen Douglas. Lincoln spoke to a crowd that evening, giving what is known today as his "house divided" speech, which can be found on PBS's Web site. "A house divided against itself cannot stand," he declared. "I believe this government cannot endure, permanently half slave and half free." Lincoln's sentiments captured the essence of the friction between the North and South. In general, the North wanted to restrict the westward expansion of slavery, while the South wanted slavery to expand.

Some historians believe that the country could not have avoided civil war. The nation had started down that path even before the first state seceded or the first shots were fired. In 1858, Republican senator William H. Seward described the North and South as two opponents, locked in a struggle to be on top. Historian Eric H. Walther details part of Seward's speech, in which the Republican said, "It is an irrepressible conflict between opposing and enduring forces and it means the United States must and will, sooner or later, become either entirely a slaveholding nation, or entirely a free-labor nation." In essence, Seward accepted Lincoln's belief that the nation could not remain divided on the issue of slavery. It is important, therefore, to examine the institution of slavery in the early years of the United States.

## THE ROOTS OF SLAVERY IN NORTH AMERICA

The institution of slavery existed throughout the colonies almost since their founding. Early records show that black slaves were being imported into the colonies as early as 1619. Colonists generally accepted slavery throughout the colonial period. Within the British Empire, slavery was legal. American colonists followed the empire, with local laws allowing for the ownership of slaves. Virginia led the way when it placed all of its laws concerning slaves into its Slave Codes in 1705.

Slavery was introduced to the English colonies in North America from the Caribbean island colonies. England, the Netherlands, France, and Spain all held colonies in the Caribbean. After the successful introduction of tobacco in Virginia, the demand for labor increased. In the seventeenth century, many planters preferred the use of indentured servants to purchasing slaves, due to high death rates among workers. An indentured servant voluntarily agreed to work for a master for an extended period of time, often about seven years in the early colonial period. As settlers tamed the land and life expectancy rose, however, indentured servants increasingly fulfilled their labor commitment and claimed their own land. Because North America seemed to have an endless amount of land, thousands left England for the New World. Dutch traders offered established planters and new landowners the same solution to their labor needs: black slaves from Africa. English traders soon followed this example, resulting in a thriving slave trade.

In the 1640s, wage levels for indentured servants began to rise sharply, and they left their masters after their terms of service were completed. However, there was no fixed term of service for slaves, who continued to serve for the remainder of their lives. Suddenly, slavery seemed like a better alternative. In 1676, Nathaniel Bacon led a disgruntled group of former indentured servants in an uprising against the ruling powers of Virginia. This uprising, called Bacon's Rebellion, convinced many that indentured servants posed more than just a financial risk to the colony. Indeed, many planters began to view slavery as a safer substitute to indentured servants who might later demand special rights or equal status with the planter class. The economics of raising tobacco made slavery an obvious choice to the question of labor needs.

In the English system of colonization, an individual or group of individuals would seek to gain title to a land grant from the Crown. If successful, these owners or administrators sought to attract planters to settle the land. Sometimes, English land owners looked to the Caribbean islands for potential settlers. Beginning in the 1660s, ambitious settlers left the Caribbean for the opportunity to claim land in southern English colonies. Because these settlers had already been using slave labor, many brought their slaves with them when they arrived in the English colonies. Tobacco reigned supreme as the cash crop in Virginia. The crop took a lot of work to manage but yielded enormous profits as European demand for tobacco rose. Needing labor, Virginia planters relied on indentured servants before finally settling on slaves.

In the North, the Puritans of New England allowed slavery, but their beliefs also recognized some slave rights. Under seventeenth-century Massachusetts code, slave owners were directly responsible for the physical and spiritual welfare of their slaves. In addition, the region's farming practices needed less manpower to produce the goods people needed. Slaves faced better circumstances living in the North than in the South. Northern inheritance laws provided for each child to inherit part of the family plot. Thus, Northern farms were smaller than Southern plantations. Consequently, the need for slave labor was greater on the large plantations than on the family farms in New England. Although slavery existed in the North, its roots were never deep.

## REVOLUTIONARY AMERICA AND SLAVERY

For many of the colonists, the Revolutionary War changed attitudes toward slavery. The revolutionary spirit made it difficult to defend slavery as an institution. After all, the Declaration of

# Presidents as Slave Owners

Many of the founders of the United States owned slaves, and 12 U.S. presidents were also slave owners. Of them, eight owned slaves *while* serving as president, including George Washington, who took some of his household slaves with him to New York and later to Philadelphia, as both cities served as the nation's capital before the creation of Washington, D.C., in 1800. Martin Van Buren seems to have owned a slave he inherited from his father. In Ulysses S. Grant's case, his wife's family owned slaves; there is one surviving record showing that Grant freed a slave in 1859.

The following is a list of presidents who held office from 1789 to 1877, and their state of residency when they were elected. The stars indicate which men owned slaves at some point in their lives and which held slaves while serving as president.

| | |
|---|---|
| 1789 to 1797 | **George Washington, Virginia |
| 1797 to 1801 | John Adams, Massachusetts |
| 1801 to 1809 | **Thomas Jefferson, Virginia |
| 1809 to 1817 | **James Madison, Virginia |
| 1817 to 1825 | **James Monroe, Virginia |
| 1825 to 1829 | John Quincy Adams, Massachusetts |
| 1829 to 1837 | **Andrew Jackson, Tennessee |
| 1837 to 1841 | *Martin Van Buren, New York |
| 1841 | *William Henry Harrison, Virginia |
| 1841 to 1845 | **John Tyler, Virginia |
| 1845 to 1849 | **James Polk, Tennessee |
| 1849 to 1850 | **Zachary Taylor, Louisiana |
| 1850 to 1853 | Millard Fillmore, New York |
| 1853 to 1857 | Franklin Pierce, New Hampshire |
| 1857 to 1861 | James Buchanan, Pennsylvania |
| 1861 to 1865 | Abraham Lincoln, Illinois |
| 1865 to 1869 | *Andrew Johnson, Tennessee |
| 1869 to 1877 | *Ulysses S. Grant, Ohio |

*Owned slaves at one time*
*** Owned slaves while serving as president*

Independence, written in 1776, declared that "all men are created equal." Thomas Jefferson, who authored the document, was himself a slave owner; yet, his original draft of the declaration accused King George III of allowing for the existence of slavery in the American colonies. Jefferson charged that, "He has waged cruel war against human nature itself, violating its most sacred rights of life and liberty in the persons of a distant people who never offended him, captivating and carrying them into slavery in another hemisphere." As historian Saul K. Padover states, "[Jefferson], the owner of more than two hundred slaves suddenly put the onus [responsibility] of slavery and the responsibility for its horrors upon the shoulders of the King of England."

Jefferson also stated that the king was "determined to keep open a market where men should be bought and sold." Although the feelings Jefferson expressed were the same ones held by many revolutionary colonists, the rebelling colonies had enough to worry about as they faced the military and naval might of Britain. Rather than risk divisions in their midst, Congress rejected the section of the declaration dealing with slaves, so as not to offend the Southern colonies of Georgia and South Carolina.

During the Revolutionary War, the British Army freed black slaves during its campaigns in the Southern colonies. The British carried out this policy because freeing slaves hurt the colonial economy, limiting the ability of Southern patriots to wage war. British military leaders believed that slaves could rise up in rebellion, though it never occurred during the war. Such a threat was more dangerous in South Carolina, where blacks outnumbered whites, and in Georgia, where slaves made up almost half of the population. British officials also hoped that policies encouraging rebellion or offering freedom to slaves would convince Southern colonists to give up their fight for independence. The strategy failed to win support, but British ships transported thousands of freed slaves out of the colonies during the war.

## THE NORTHWEST TERRITORY

After winning its independence, the young United States faced many challenges. Power lay at the state level and the new national government lacked financial stability. The federal government wanted to sell western lands, but several of the original 13 states claimed ownership of these lands. The west-ward movement of settlers forced the federal and state governments to deal with the issue of title to western lands and slavery in those lands.

In 1787, the Congress of the Confederation passed the Northwest Ordinance. Under this law, states gave up their claims to western lands to the national government. More important, the Northwest Ordinance set the example that the federal government, not the individual states, governed matters having to do with the territories. This law defined the Northwest Territory as the lands north of the Ohio River, east of the Mississippi River, and south of the Great Lakes. Through the Northwest Ordinance, Congress established the process by which western lands were organized into territories before being admitted as states. Congress organized a region into a territory, appointing the governor and other officials of the territory. (Later, Congress amended the process, allowing the president to appoint the governor, depending on Senate approval.) The Northwest Ordinance set a minimum population in a territory before organizing a legislature (5,000) and applying for statehood (60,000). The ordinance required the Northwest Territory to generate a minimum of three and a maximum of five future states. In time, five states were carved out of the territory: Ohio, Indiana, Illinois, Michigan, and Wisconsin.

A key aspect of the Northwest Ordinance was its handling of slavery. The legislative act stated: "There shall be neither slavery nor involuntary servitude in the said territory, other-wise than in the punishment of crime. . . ." The condition was remarkable, especially when one considers that slavery was

*In 1676, a young Virginia farmer named Nathaniel Bacon led an uprising against the colonial governor of Virginia. Supported by frustrated indentured servants, Bacon's Rebellion seized control of Jamestown, the capital of the colony, and burned it down* (above). *This harrowing experience caused Virginia planters to turn from indentured servitude to slavery.*

allowed in some of the Northern states at the time. The ordinance prohibited slavery in an area where future U.S. expansion was certain to reach. Thus, several of the free states of the North were without slavery from the very beginning, when they became territories. After the approval of the U.S. Constitution, the new federal Congress adopted the laws and ordinances of the Congress of the Confederation, which meant the provisions of the Northwest Ordinance remained in effect. Later legislation, most notably the Missouri Compromise (1820), effectively extended free territory west of the Mississippi River in much the same way that the Northwest Ordinance had done east of it.

## SLAVERY AS A STATE ISSUE

After the country declared its independence from Britain in 1776, slavery was a state matter. After independence, Northern states began to emancipate their slaves, beginning with Vermont in 1777. By 1800, each of the Northern states had banned slavery. The idea of freeing slaves was a new one, standing in sharp contrast to European practices and thinking. The influences of the Quakers and the Puritans (two religious groups) in the North fed the desire to end slavery. The movement did not catch on in Northern politics, however. Indeed, as late as 1818, the state of Illinois almost included a provision in its state constitution allowing slavery. Nevertheless, after 1820, slavery in the United States was mostly found only in the states south of the Ohio River. Slavery had become an institution peculiar to the South.

## THE U.S. CONSTITUTION AND SLAVERY

The U.S. Constitution does not specifically mention the word *slavery*, though the document does refer to it in three places. The first, found in Article I, Section 2, involves representation in Congress. The Constitution sets the number of representatives for each state in the House of Representatives and charges direct taxes based on the population of free persons (including indentured servants) and "three-fifths of all other Persons." This "three-fifths clause" required a compromise during the Constitutional Convention. Northerners were willing to consider slaves as property, but wanted them to play no role in population. On the other hand, Southerners wanted slaves to count for population purposes, but not for taxes. The convention delegates used the ratio of three-fifths in determining the population and taxable value of slaves; this meant that slaves were counted as three-fifths of a person. Under the three-fifths compromise, Northerners indirectly recognized slavery. The same clause specifically excluded Native Americans from population counts.

Also, in Article I, Section 9, the Constitution deals with the slave trade. Many wanted the new Constitution to ban the slave trade, but state conventions needed to ratify (approve) the new federal government. Convention delegates understood that the slave trade needed to end, but also recognized that such an outright prohibition would probably lead several states to reject the proposed constitution. Consequently, the convention compromised by ensuring that Congress could not end the slave trade before 1808, or 20 years after the convention. Thus, the slave trade continued, but the convention also agreed upon a timeline for its demise. The compromise appeased both sides, and Congress passed a law in 1807 that ended the slave trade on January 1, 1808.

The last mention of slavery in the Constitution is found in Article IV, Section 2. Under the terms of this passage, states had an obligation to return fugitive slaves. Indeed, the Constitution requires that states return fugitives held to "Service or Labour in one State" to the "Party to whom such Service or Labour may be due." In other words, an escaped slave (or indentured servant) did not achieve freedom by fleeing to another state, since the Constitution did not allow a state to override the obligations of an individual in another state. Because states wrote their own slave codes, the fugitive-slave clause kept the different state laws from denying any slave owner his rights to his legal property (slaves).

# American Slavery

At the close of the eighteenth century, slavery in the United States appeared to be dying out. The Constitution allowed Congress to end the slave trade, a virtual certainty even during ratification. More important, the price of tobacco plummeted at the very time that U.S. production of the crop fell due to worn-out soil. Slavery in the South faced the inevitable fate of extinction already underway in the North. Then, in 1793, an unlikely source showed the new economic potential for slavery.

Eli Whitney was an inventor from New England. Whitney toured the South in 1792, traveling through Georgia and South Carolina. On his journey, Whitney observed the problems facing Southern planters. He took particular note of their cotton production. Raw cotton is a fluffy fiber containing seeds. The fiber is useless until the seeds are removed. Such a process required labor, and lots of it. Whitney designed and created a cotton engine, called a cotton gin. The cotton gin was made up of a series of brushes attached to mechanical wheels, which pulled the cotton through the brushes and wire screens, filtering out the seeds in the process. Whitney's cotton gin was hand-powered and allowed just a few workers to remove seeds from cotton in a fraction of the time it took to accomplish the same task by hand.

Almost immediately, Southerners began copying Whitney's design. Cotton production soared. The profitability of a cotton cash crop came just as tobacco profits fell, thus paving the way for slavery to continue in the South. Cotton production doubled each decade after 1800 until 1860. By 1840, Southern plantations produced about 75 percent of the world's cotton. By mid-century, cotton was the largest U.S. export. Cotton and slavery were now an important foundation of the national economy. The importance of cotton and slavery to the Southern economy made the slave issue a sensitive one for many Southerners. Consequently, many in the South wanted to protect slavery from both external and internal threats.

## SLAVE REBELLIONS

In the early republic, two major slave rebellions spawned fear in the South. The first was a rebellion planned by Gabriel Prosser, a slave from Virginia. Prosser planned to lead a revolt into Richmond on August 30, 1800. Heavy rains forced Prosser to delay his plans for another day, but in the meantime, two slaves told their master of the planned rebellion. Virginia governor James Monroe called out the state militia to squelch the uprising. Prosser initially escaped, but a fellow slave turned him in. The state of Virginia tried Gabriel Prosser and many others, including two of Prosser's brothers. Upon conviction, Prosser, his two brothers, and 24 other slaves were hanged for their parts in the conspiracy. Amazingly, Virginia executed the men not for what they had done, but for what they intended to do.

The Prosser Rebellion had demonstrated what slaves might do. Southern planters feared a slave rebellion. This resulted in more restrictive slave laws. Prosser had enjoyed freedom of movement among plantations, allowing him to plan the rebellion with many slaves in different places. Following the uproar, most states and/or slave owners limited the rights of slaves to travel. Virginia later banned the education of slaves and restricted their movement by outlawing the practice of hiring out one's slaves to do work away from their plantation.

The state of Virginia had more free blacks than any other Southern state. Many of these free blacks had been released by their masters because of the ideals of the Revolutionary War. Free blacks served as a constant reminder of the inconsistency of black slavery. Virginia could not afford to have large numbers of free blacks reminding slaves of the life denied them. Within a few years of Prosser's Rebellion, Virginia took the extraordinary step of forcing free blacks to leave the state or again become slaves.

The most notorious slave rebellion in the pre–Civil War South was the Nat Turner Rebellion in 1831. Nat Turner was a slave from Southampton County, Virginia, a region in which black slaves outnumbered whites. On August 21, 1831, Turner led several other slaves from plantation house to plantation house, killing whites and freeing slaves. The rebels showed no favoritism, killing all whites they encountered, regardless of age or gender. At the start of their killing spree, Turner and his followers used axes, hatchets, knives, and other non-firearm weapons in order to avoid detection. As Turner's band moved from plantation to plantation, the size of the rebel group grew to more than 50 people.

By the time a white militia challenged the rebellion two days after it began, Turner and his rebels had killed at least 57 white men, women, and children. The militia's resistance ended the rebellion, but Turner escaped. He avoided capture for more than two months, until a local farmer found him hiding in a cave on October 30. Turner did not have to wait long for his trial.

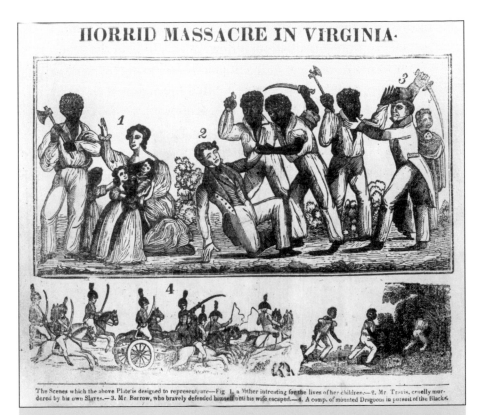

HORRID MASSACRE IN VIRGINIA.

The Scenes which the above Plate is designed to represent are—Fig 1. a Mother intreating for the lives of her children.—2. Mr. Travis, cruelly murdered by his own Slaves.—3. Mr. Barrow, who bravely defended himself until his wife escaped.—4. A comp. of mounted Dragoons in pursuit of the Blacks.

*Led by a young slave prone to prophetic visions, Nat Turner's Rebellion in 1831 ended with the deaths of at least 57 white men, women, and children. One of the most brutal slave uprisings in U.S. history, this revolt also resulted in many slaves being wrongly accused of conspiring with Turner. The differences between the North and South flared up when news of the rebellion spread throughout the country, causing even further damage to the relationship between the two regions. Above, a newspaper illustration depicts the Nat Turner Rebellion.*

On November 5, a Virginia court tried and convicted Turner of insurrection (rebellion against authority). Turner received a sentence of death, and the execution by hanging was carried out on November 11.

The results of the Nat Turner Rebellion were even more drastic than the results of the Prosser Rebellion three decades earlier. Southern states imposed even more restrictions on slaves. Southern fears of slave rebellions were now based upon a real example of violence against whites.

Equally important, some Northerners viewed slavery as unjust. The Turner Rebellion helped rouse concerns about slavery. Northern antislavery groups began attracting more support, while Southern antislavery feeling virtually disappeared due to widespread fear across the South. The result was that abolitionism became, almost exclusively, a Northern movement. The differing attitudes toward slavery helped create a wider divide between the two sections of the nation.

## THE MISSOURI COMPROMISE

In 1819, passions flared over the issue of slavery when Missouri applied for U.S. statehood. Slavery was firmly established in the area, with the institution dating back to French and Spanish rule of the vast Louisiana Territory, later renamed Missouri Territory. When Thomas Jefferson purchased Louisiana from France in 1803, the United States guaranteed property rights of all citizens within the territory. In 1819, the Missouri Territory had a population of about 60,000 people, including 10,000 slaves. While Congress deliberated on whether to grant statehood to Missouri, an area carved out of the territory, a New York representative named James Tallmadge offered an amendment that produced an explosive controversy.

The Tallmadge Amendment set it so that Missouri would enter the Union as a slave state, but arranged for the eventual end of slavery there. Under the Tallmadge Amendment, no one could legally bring new slaves into the state. Southerners were outraged over the amendment, with many viewing it as an attempt by the federal government to limit property rights. Northerners generally favored the amendment, some for moral and humanitarian reasons, and others for political purposes.

It is important to recognize the political landscape into which Tallmadge put forward his proposal. Alabama had been the twenty-second state to enter the Union. Upon Alabama's admission, there were an equal number of slave and free states. Thus, both free and slave states held equal power in the U.S. Senate. The addition of another slave state threatened to tip the balance of power to the slave states. Although many in the North were not abolitionists, they were opposed to the idea of the slaveholding states expanding their national power.

Northerners held up Missouri's application, and Congress debated how to handle the situation. While the debate over Missouri continued to rage, another application for statehood further muddied the situation. Maine, a territory owned by Massachusetts, applied for admission into the Union. Massachusetts had supported the separation of Maine, but only if the country accepted Maine as a state before March 4, 1820. Otherwise, the territory would remain part of Massachusetts. Southerners were irritated with Northern attempts to block Missouri statehood and support the Tallmadge Amendment, and they promised to block Maine's application.

Both sides were stuck, until Speaker of the House Henry Clay took the lead. Clay reminded Northerners that if they held on to the Tallmadge Amendment, then Southerners had the necessary votes to deny Maine's application. He also told Southerners that unless Maine entered the nation as a free state, Northern votes would prevent Missouri from achieving statehood. A few Northern senators changed their stance and voted with their Southern colleagues to kill the Tallmadge Amendment. Clay's authority helped forge the compromise.

The Senate recognized that the two measures needed support from both the North and the South and included both statehood applications into one bill, thereby linking the two applications. Finally, the Senate also included a provision whereby slavery was prohibited north of the 36° 30' north parallel (the southern boundary of Missouri in the original Louisiana Purchase) with the exception of Missouri. This line had been drawn in earlier Senate versions of the bill, but the House of Representatives, dominated by Northerners, had voted to reject it. Thus, under the Senate version, the Tallmadge Amendment was removed, Maine entered as a free state (1820), Missouri entered as a slave state (1821), and slavery was banned north of 36° 30'. This piece of legislation became known as the Compromise of 1820, or the Missouri Compromise.

The compromise was a feat of political leadership, especially for Henry Clay, who successfully steered it through the House of Representatives. For his efforts, Clay became a national figure in U.S. politics, leading and influencing national policy for the next 30 years. Nationalists cheered the agreement, believing that it signaled the end to threats of disunity. There were others, however, including former president Thomas Jefferson, who believed the compromise would hurt the nation rather than help it. The elder statesman included his objections to the deal in a letter to John Holmes. Author William Chauncey Fowler quotes Jefferson's letter:

> . . . but this momentous question, like a fire bell in the night, awakened and filled me with terror. I considered it at once as the knell of the Union. It is hushed indeed for the moment. But this is a reprieve only, not a final sentence. A geographical line, coinciding with a marked principle, moral and political, once conceived and held up to the angry passions of men, will never be obliterated; and every new irritation will mark it deeper and deeper.

In Jefferson's eyes, the Missouri Compromise only served short-term political interests. The long-term effect of the legislation would surely lead to future arguments over the merits of slavery since the nation was likely to continue expanding westward.

The Missouri Compromise delayed the issue of slavery until both sections of the country were more committed to settling the matter, regardless of cost. Indeed, although the compromise avoided the breakup of the Union, it also uncovered the deep division separating the North and the South. By compromising, both sides had avoided eroding the Union. But westward expansion in the coming years virtually guaranteed the issue would again threaten the unity of the young nation.

The Missouri Compromise also affected the party system. The Federalist Party fell apart following the 1816 elections, and James Monroe, running unopposed, won his second presidential term in 1820. The compromise was struck in the midst of the so-called Era of Good Feelings, leading many to believe the deal had ended all debate on the issue of slavery.

But the remaining party, the Democratic-Republicans, began to splinter into two, in large part over the North-South issues that slavery had exposed. Jackson's Democrat Party emphasized the idea of states' rights while the National Republicans favored a stronger federal government. The latter party later became the Whig Party during Jackson's second term, 1833 to 1837. The compromise also drew attention to the fragile balance between slave and free states in the Senate. Keeping this balance of power became a key goal to many in the coming years. Such a goal often served to emphasize the differences between the two regions. Arkansas entered as a slave state in 1836, followed the next year by Michigan, a free state. Yet, there was a limited availability of useable lands for slave territories, meaning the free states eventually gained the upper hand in the Senate.

Finally, the compromise is significant for at least one other reason: It marked the first time since the ratification of the Constitution that Congress banned slavery from public territory. In spite of the compromise, public opinion in the North began to shift against slavery. The abolitionist movement helped to change attitudes about slavery.

## ABOLITIONISM

The antislavery movement had been spreading in Europe and the United States since before the Revolutionary War. European efforts to end slavery continued to increase throughout the final decades of the eighteenth century. In the early years of the nine-teenth century, antislavery forces scored a huge victory when England ended its participation in the international slave trade. During that time, effective on January 1, 1808, Congress banned the importation of slaves. In Europe, the victories provided a push to antislavery groups to do more than just end the slave trade. Groups began calling for the abolition of slavery.

Despite the increase of antislavery groups in Europe, the American antislavery movement followed a different course in its growth. In the United States, many Americans were against slavery, but they did not become a political force until the early 1830s. Then, the climate changed as the voice of the movement shifted from being only against slavery to being firmly in favor of abolition.

Many of the antislavery organizations in the United States in the early nineteenth century were committed to removing blacks from the United States. These groups often opposed slav-ery on moral grounds, but favored gradual emancipation. Many Americans frowned on slavery, but they were unsure what to do with freed slaves. The popular solution was to gather free blacks and ship them to Africa or some other place removed from the United States. Most of the organizations in favor of this solution, such as the American Colonization Society, did not challenge the legality of slavery. Instead, most efforts included compen-sation to slave owners. Beginning in the 1820s, several groups of free blacks were shipped to the west coast of Africa, where the colonists founded the independent black republic of Libe-ria, which means "land of the free." Despite colonization efforts, there were more slaves and blacks in the United States than any organization could have relocated to Africa. Besides, many of the free blacks wanted to stay in North America, where most of their families had lived for several generations.

By 1830, the passive antislavery movement, which focused on colonization, was in decline. At almost the same time, the

As more people became aware of the evils of slavery, they began to organize into groups calling for its end. Known as abolitionists, these people worked to educate the public and push the issue to the forefront of national politics. Determined anti-slavery activist William Lloyd Garrison helped to develop the Underground Railroad. He also published abolitionist newspapers, such as the influential publication The Liberator.

need and value of slaves to the economy of the Deep South was becoming increasingly clear. The antislavery movement needed a new vision and new leadership. Stepping into that role was a fearless and uncompromising editor named William Lloyd Garrison.

Born in 1805 in Massachusetts, the teenaged Garrison was apprenticed to learn the printing trade. Garrison learned the newspaper business and grew to despise slavery. After working for a moderate antislavery newspaper, the young printer decided to put his talents to use for a greater cause. Garrison ended up in Boston, where in 1831 he founded the antislavery newspaper *The Liberator*. Garrison was the most outspoken critic of U.S. slavery throughout the 1830s. Author Diane Ravitch recalls Garrison's statement from his first issue of *The Liberator*, in which he declared:

> I am aware that many object to the severity of my language; but is there not cause for severity? I will be as harsh as truth, and as uncompromising as justice. On this subject, I do not wish to think, or to speak, or write, with moderation. No! no! Tell a man whose house is on fire to give a moderate alarm; tell him to moderately rescue his wife from the hands of the ravisher; tell the mother to gradually extricate her babe from the fire into which it has fallen;—but urge me not to use moderation in a cause like the present. I am in earnest—I will not equivocate—I will not excuse—I will not retreat a single inch—AND I WILL BE HEARD.

In his radical publication, Garrison demanded the immediate emancipation of all African-American slaves without payment to their owners. He refused to accept anything less than the rapid abolition of slavery. His uncompromising demands split the abolitionist movement. The radical wing demanded immediate abolition of slavery. The moderate wing opposed slavery, but stopped short of abolition. Thus, *abolitionism* usually

# The Underground Railroad

The U.S. Constitution, ratified in 1788, required individuals and states to return escaped slaves to their owners. The federal government enacted fugitive slave laws guaranteeing the property rights of slave owners. The Underground Railroad, however, offered some slaves hope of a free life. The Underground Railroad was an informal network of people, routes, locations, and resources to help fleeing slaves escape to the free states of the North and to Canada. Abolitionists, free blacks, and Christians, especially the Quakers, worked together to assist fugitive slaves.

In a literal sense, the Underground Railroad was neither underground nor a railroad. *Underground* referred to the secretive nature of the activities, which were illegal under federal law. The term *railroad* was used since much of the network terminology was patterned on railroad jargon. For example, individuals who helped slaves find the railroad were "agents" and guides were "conductors." People called "stationmasters" hid "cargo" (escaped slaves) in their homes or other places called "stations," and "stockholders" were those who helped fund the efforts. All of these were common railroad terms.

Many prominent Americans helped support the Underground Railroad, including Levi Coffin, a Quaker who helped more than 3,000 people escape slavery, and Ohioan John Fairfield, whose parents owned slaves. Harriet Tubman was perhaps the most celebrated worker on the Underground Railroad. Tubman was herself an escaped slave who made at least 19 trips back into the South and helped lead more than 300 slaves to freedom. Some called her "Moses," as a tribute to her commitment to free her people from slavery. Tubman later aided the Union war effort, providing information about the lay of the land to Union commanders and nursing the wounded. Following the war, Tubman supported women's suffrage and helped found a home for poor elderly blacks.

refers to the smaller, radical element of the movement, while *antislavery* refers to the larger, moderate group.

Garrison labored virtually alone in his war to end slavery. Many Americans disliked slavery, but few were abolitionists in the 1830s. Most Americans were not ready for such a radical, uncompromising approach to the slavery issue. Instead, the moderates within the movement generally favored gradual emancipation. This part of the movement eventually found its way into the Republican Party after the party's founding in 1854. Like the Republican Party platform, these moderates opposed the extension of slavery in the territories, but did not demand the abolition of the "peculiar institution." Thus, Garrison's real contributions came in the rise of abolitionist sentiment, which led to increased tensions between North and South. These rising tensions eventually helped spark the Civil War, which, in turn, resulted in the abolition of slavery in the United States.

## ELIJAH LOVEJOY

Another early abolitionist, Elijah Lovejoy, faced fierce opposition to his views on slavery. The Maine native moved to St. Louis in 1827, and worked there as a Presbyterian minister and editor of a weekly religious newspaper. He wrote a number of editorials critical of slavery and religions other than his own, upsetting some of the local elite. In May 1836, Lovejoy wrote an editorial criticizing a local judge for failing to allow charges against whites who had stirred up a mob and lynched a free black man living in the area. Influential local leaders and others he had offended forced Lovejoy to leave town.

He moved to Alton, another Illinois community, where he became the editor of a local paper, the *Alton Observer*. Lovejoy continued to publish his abolitionist ideas and beliefs, leading many pro-slavery groups in the area to challenge him. Three times, pro-slavery mobs destroyed his printing press in order to silence him. Three times, Lovejoy purchased new equipment.

Once again, on November 7, 1837, a pro-slavery crowd gathered to destroy Lovejoy's printing press. This time, the abolitionist tried to defend his property. Members of the mob shot and killed Lovejoy before throwing his press into the Mississippi River.

Elijah Lovejoy, a white Northerner living in a free state, had been killed for speaking out against black slavery. Abolitionists across the nation depicted Lovejoy as a martyr, a person who dies for his beliefs or for a cause. According to author Arnold Whitridge,

> The murder of Elijah Lovejoy made far more converts to abolitionism than Garrison's editorials in *The Liberator*, and the attack on Charles Sumner in the Senate, John Brown's massacre of innocent men in Kansas, and the raid on Harper's Ferry all contributed to the growing feeling, originally confined to the extremists, that the time had come for the two sections of the country to separate.

Indeed, the issue of slavery was beginning to affect more than just Southerners and slaves. Americans from all parts of the nation were beginning to wrestle with the issue in ways that were more personal. The intensity of emotions over the topic only became stronger during the 1840s and 1850s.

## UNCLE TOM'S CABIN

In the early 1850s, author Harriet Beecher Stowe made antislavery fashionable. Her novel *Uncle Tom's Cabin* depicted the harsh realities of slave life. The work was antislavery in tone, portraying how slave owners had the power to sell members of a slave family. *Uncle Tom's Cabin* was a publishing success, selling more than 300,000 copies in the United States during the first year of its publication. The book helped to shift public opinion against slavery. Many historians believe that the book helped energize the abolitionist and antislavery causes of the 1850s. Many in the North applauded the work, while many in

*An unwavering abolitionist and newspaper editor, Elijah Lovejoy fearlessly published his honest opinions regarding biased and discriminatory behavior. In response, mobs of angry slavery supporters repeatedly destroyed Lovejoy's printing presses. Their protests resulted in Lovejoy's death, which convinced more people in the North to join the antislavery movement.*

the South and pro-slavery advocates criticized both the author and her novel.

## SOUTHERN DEFENSE OF SLAVERY

The Southern attitude toward slavery prior to 1830 often mirrored that of Northerners, viewing slavery as evil, but necessary. Just as abolitionist societies were rising in the North, however, business profits in the South were also rising, made possible by slave-produced cotton. As abolitionists raised their voices ever louder, Southerners stated their arguments to justify the "peculiar institution."

For instance, South Carolinian John C. Calhoun was a prominent states' rights advocate and staunch supporter of slavery who changed his views on slavery over the course of his political career. Historian Arnold Whitridge notes two of Calhoun's statements on slavery, one as a young man and another when he was older. As a young man, Calhoun described slavery as "a dark cloud that obscures half the luster of our free institutions." Later in life, Calhoun said, "Many in the South once believed that it was a moral and political evil; that folly and delusion are now gone; we now see it in its true light, and regard it as the most safe and stable basis for free institutions in the world." Calhoun's views on slavery evolved from a certain level of shame to outright pride. Whereas before Calhoun had apologized for the presence of slavery, he later insisted that slavery was beneficial to the American way of life. What makes this transformation remarkable is that in both statements, Calhoun explains the effect of slavery on free institutions, or free society. The avid advocate for states' rights did not just believe that the benefits outweighed the shame of slavery. Instead, Calhoun came to believe that slavery in and of itself was good.

Calhoun's attitudes reflect the changing views of many Southerners, who believed in the necessity of slavery. Over time, the South was no longer content to allow others to question the morality of slavery. Instead, many in the South wanted others to see slavery as a benefit to the nation. Meanwhile, many Northerners found it increasingly difficult to tolerate such attitudes. The two sections of the country were growing further apart on an issue that seemed unlikely to fade.

During the 1830s and 1840s, there were several clues that the Union was in danger of splitting. In particular, the South appeared increasingly less tolerant of any criticism of slavery. In

1835, an incident in Charleston, South Carolina, raised tensions over antislavery printed materials. A mob seized and destroyed abolitionist literature in the Charleston post office. Following the incident, Southern postmasters rarely delivered antislavery mail. Even the House of Representatives fell to Southern pressures to no longer discuss slavery, adopting the so-called "gag rule" in 1836. Under this rule, members of Congress could not discuss slavery during debate. Instead, Congress postponed all antislavery resolutions, petitions, or amendments before any were even read on the House floor. Former president John Quincy Adams, who was elected to the House following his presidency, led others in overturning the gag rule in 1844. By the 1850s, Southern defense of slavery was becoming ever more heated.

As historian Reginald Stuart explains, the South "defended this institution on cultural as well as economic and constitutional grounds" to preserve their regional culture. From the Southern viewpoint, the United States needed to acquire more territory in order for the South to maintain its unique culture. Thus, Southerners came to believe that if the United States ceased to expand and gain new territories, then slavery would soon die out, killing the Southern way of life.

As the presidential election of 1860 loomed, the issue of slavery weighed heavily on the hearts and minds of many Americans. Instead of disappearing, slavery continued to rear its head as a continual reminder of the stark differences between the North and the South. By 1860, there were 31 million Americans, 4 million of whom were slaves. In the 1850s, the difficulties surrounding slavery, abolition, and western territories could not be ignored any longer.

# Nullification
# and States' Rights

Another one of the underlying causes of the Civil War involves states' rights. Advocates of states' rights emphasize the power of states to determine matters for themselves, as opposed to the federal government making such decisions. In essence, the debate over states' rights centers on who has sovereignty, or power—each individual state or the national government.

President Andrew Jackson, who held office from 1829 to 1837, tended to favor the rights and powers of the states over that of the national government. He reacted strongly against his critics and political opponents. As president, Jackson faced an opponent from within his own party serving in his administration: Vice President John C. Calhoun.

A South Carolina native, Calhoun was 46 years old when Jackson took office and already had considerable experience in the national government. The Southerner was a former member of Congress, had served as secretary of war for eight years, and was the sitting vice president, having served under John Quincy

Adams. A devoted public servant, Calhoun seemed like the perfect man to partner with Jackson—but Calhoun's views on a key issue had evolved over the years.

One crucial issue was the national tariff. A tariff is a tax placed on goods imported from other countries. The purposes of the tax are to collect money for the government and raise the price of foreign products in order to help domestic industries. This was a key policy that helped manufacturing industries in the early republic and supplied the new government with its largest source of income. Calhoun had once been a strong supporter of the 1816 national tariff, which added a 25 percent tax to various manufactured goods. His opinion shifted, though, as he observed the results of these policies on his native state. Over the next several years, Congress gradually raised the tariff rates.

The Tariff of 1828 was almost more than Calhoun and many other Southerners could tolerate. The tariff was raised on imported textiles, manufactured goods, and a variety of raw materials produced in the West. The new tariffs were as high as 50 percent on some items. The South believed it saw no direct benefit from the tariff. The only items protected by the tariff were items the South did not produce. Because tariffs allowed domestic producers to charge more for their products, Southerners understandably felt cheated. They believed the Tariff of 1828 was outrageous, calling it the "Tariff of Abominations."

Opponents of the tariff found a willing and capable ally in Calhoun. He was an avid supporter of states' rights and he opposed the tariff. Calhoun put together a constitutional theory whereby states could exercise their rights over the power and authority of the federal government. Calhoun's political views gave him the role of the nation's most important advocate for states' rights. In 1816, Calhoun believed that the manufacturing industries needed protection in order to support themselves. He also believed the industries were crucial to national defense. A decade later, however, Calhoun and others considered the industries strong enough to stand without government protection.

Calhoun was a South Carolina man. The economy of his home state was agriculturally based, founded upon the slave system. South Carolina produced things such as cotton, indigo, and rice, but not manufactured items. In fact, the state had to import virtually all of the goods it needed. Because all of these goods came either from the North or from other countries, a state like South Carolina carried most of the weight of the national tariff. Likewise, tariffs on manufactured cloth indirectly hurt South Carolina. When U.S. tariffs increased the tax on textiles, foreign buyers purchased less raw cotton from the South because they knew they would sell less of their product within the United States. The economic realities of American tariff policies led many Southerners to support states' rights. Some even suggested secession.

In 1828, Calhoun did not support secession. After all, he was the vice president of the United States, standing for reelection. Still, like his fellow South Carolinians, Calhoun shared many of the same frustrations with federal policy. South Carolina insisted on its rights as a state. To assert these rights, Calhoun claimed that states held the power of *nullification*, the refusal of a state government to adopt a federal law.

Calhoun and other Southerners opposed the tariff for various reasons. Not the least among these were the changing economies of the North and South. The Northern economy increasingly relied upon manufacturing, which the tariff policy helped promote and protect. In contrast, the Southern economy, especially in the Deep South, relied upon slave labor.

Slavery in the border states continued to decline; indeed, the numbers of slaves in some of the border states (Missouri, Kentucky, Maryland, and Delaware) had dropped each decade since the founding of the new government. Calhoun understood that if the border states became economically tied to the

John C. Calhoun, a Southern politician and future vice president, was a strong supporter of states' rights and slavery. The senator from South Carolina vigorously fought against tariff increases that benefited the North but were detrimental to the Southern economy. His early efforts to withdraw South Carolina from the Union foreshadowed the upcoming dispute over states' rights, one of the causes of the Civil War.

North, then slavery was likely to decrease or even disappear. If slavery faded in the Upper South, slave states would lose their political allies in the national government. Without their political allies, free states might begin to threaten the existence of slavery in the Deep South. Such a shift posed a grave threat to a state like South Carolina, since its economy was dependent upon slave labor. This realization led many Southern political leaders to demand later that there be no restrictions on slavery in the western territories. In the 1820s and 1830s, Calhoun and others directed their energies into repealing the tariff, since that was the most visible example of the national government exercising its power over the states.

Calhoun saw tariffs as a means by which the federal government took Southern wealth and redistributed it to Northern manufacturers. In other words, Congress asserted federal power in order to benefit one section of the country at the expense of another. The vice president claimed that Congress only had the authority to pass laws that served to benefit the whole nation, not just one section. Calhoun argued that states held the power in the U.S. political system. The states created the national government, which included Congress and the Supreme Court. Consequently, the states held the power to determine whether a particular federal law was appropriate.

Calhoun did not believe Congress or the Supreme Court could make such a determination, since they were established by the states. Instead, if a state questioned whether a law was constitutional, then the state could step in and block the law. In order to accomplish this, the people in a state could hold a convention. Such a convention could examine a federal law and declare it invalid within that state. Calhoun then argued that the law would remain canceled within that state unless three-fourths of the states ratified an amendment to the U.S. Constitution expressly giving Congress authority to legislate on the matter contained within the federal law.

Then, Calhoun spelled out that the state had choices: either yield to the will of the nation or secede from the United States. The vice president thought that any law that favored one section of the country over another was unconstitutional. He also believed that if each state held the power to veto national laws, then federal taxes would be fairer to the different sections of the country. The South Carolina legislature published Calhoun's theory of nullification in 1828. Because Calhoun held a national office, he insisted the pamphlet be published anonymously.

## The Mason-Dixon Line

Where exactly is the line between the North and South? Throughout the first half of the nineteenth century, many politicians referred to the Mason-Dixon Line as the boundary separating the two sections. This famous line was established in order to settle a boundary dispute that originated in the seventeenth century. The disagreement started after King Charles I issued a land grant in 1632 to Maryland founder George Calvert, and King Charles II issued a conflicting grant in 1682 to Pennsylvania founder William Penn.

The inconsistent boundaries led to confusion, resulting in the Calvert and Penn families taking the matter to court. In 1750, England's chief justice ruled that the boundary between Pennsylvania and Maryland should be located 15 miles (24 kilometers) south of Philadelphia. The two sides continued to wrangle over the decision, but in 1760, both families agreed to the proposed line.

However, no colonial surveyors had enough experience to tackle the sensitive assignment of finding and marking the border. Instead, two English experts came to North America to do the job. Charles Mason was an astronomer working at the Royal Society in

The vice president's ideas of nullification appealed to many in South Carolina. Calhoun himself, however, did not desire that South Carolina or any state nullify a federal law. Instead, the vice president hoped that his theory would convince President Jackson to pressure Congress to reduce tariffs. Jackson's idea of loyalty, however, was that his fellow government leaders should not criticize him, as Calhoun was doing. Jackson interpreted Calhoun's actions as disloyal, leading to a widening divide between the two men. Throughout Jackson's first term in office (1829–1833), Calhoun continued to lose influence within the

Greenwich, England. Jeremiah Dixon was a well-known surveyor from Durham County, England. The two arrived in Philadelphia in November 1763 to begin their work. The process took about five years to complete.

Mason and Dixon used stars to calculate the boundary, which represented the line between Pennsylvania and Maryland, as well as the boundary between Maryland and Delaware. At every mile, Mason and Dixon laid down stone markers that had been shipped from England, with more elaborate stones every 5 miles (8 km). Many of these stones still survive today and they indicate the legal boundary. Modern GPS surveys have shown that Mason and Dixon were remarkably accurate in their placement of the stones, only missing the true line by as little as 1 inch (2.5 centimeters) or as much as 800 feet (243 meters).

To define the boundaries of slavery in the western territories, the 1820 Missouri Compromise used the Mason-Dixon Line, extending it westward to the Ohio River until it emptied into the Mississippi River, then west along the famed 36° 30' line. Though changed a little from the original line in the East, many called this new boundary between slave and free states the Mason-Dixon Line. Delaware, although it was a slave state according to the line, remained in the Union during the Civil War. The Mason-Dixon Line symbolized the cultural divide between the North and South.

administration. Instead, Jackson increasingly turned to a strong nationalist named Martin Van Buren for advice. During the second year of Jackson's presidency, the debate over states' rights heated up in the U.S. Senate.

## THE WEBSTER-HAYNE DEBATE

One of the most critical and celebrated Senate debates took place in January 1830. As the Senate considered policy concerning federal lands in the West, a Connecticut senator proposed suspending all federal-land sales. One of President Jackson's allies, Thomas Hart Benton of Missouri, immediately argued against the suggestion, claiming that such a move was simply a way by which New England could keep workers in Northeastern factories and limit prosperity in the West.

After Benton spoke, a young senator from South Carolina named Robert Y. Hayne continued the argument. Hayne advocated an alliance between the South and the West: The South could support the West against suspending land sales and the West could support the South against the tariffs. Hayne argued that both the tariffs and the proposal to suspend the land sales were designed to help only one section of the country: the North. The South Carolinian maintained that land sales should be an issue for individual states, not the federal government.

The next day, Massachusetts senator Daniel Webster answered Hayne in a lengthy speech, but he did not deal directly with the question of western lands and tariffs. Instead, the Massachusetts senator addressed the issues of states' rights and the power of the national government. Webster argued that the North was a true friend to the West. He also stated his support for federal principles over the economic gain of one region of the nation. Finally, Webster criticized the idea of states' rights over the authority of the federal government. John C. Calhoun, who as U.S. vice president served as the president of the Senate, discussed the situation with Hayne. The senator from South

*In 1830, senators Daniel Webster and Robert Hayne participated in one of the most eventful debates in U.S. history. Hayne, a South Carolinian, argued for the South and the newer territories of the West to join forces against tariffs and a suspension of land sales perceived to benefit only the North. New Englander Webster (above) did not address these issues but instead fought for the preservation of the Union.*

Carolina defended the theory of nullification. The next two afternoons, Webster again took the floor of the Senate to respond to Hayne. His response is known as his "Second Reply to Hayne." Webster argued that the will of the people was more important than that of the states. As author Kevin Julius recorded, Webster declared, "It is, Sir, the people's Constitution, the people's government, made for the people, made by the people, and answerable to the people." Later Webster ended his speech by proclaiming, "Liberty and Union, now and for ever, one and inseparable!"

The speech mesmerized many in the North. Within a few months, 40,000 copies of the speech had been sold. Future American leaders read the speech, and many American school-children memorized it. The Webster-Hayne debate revealed some of the underlying differences between the two sections of the nation. Although mostly unseen, these differences contin-ued to grow more explosive in the coming years.

## THE NULLIFICATION CRISIS

More than two and a half years passed with no significant prog-ress made on the issues exposed by the Webster-Hayne debate. Southern states wanted Congress to throw out the Tariff of 1828, but the tariff remained. President Jackson called on Con-gress to provide some sort of tariff relief, and Congress took up the issue, passing another tariff bill in 1832. The new tariff law lowered taxes on many items, but actually increased the rates on manufactured cloth and iron. South Carolina decided it was time to take action. Some South Carolinians wanted to rebel against the federal government. Calhoun offered his leadership to calm the situation. The vice president now openly embraced nullification as an alternative to secession. His home state lis-tened to him, and in the 1832 elections the citizens voted in a majority of legislators who favored nullification.

The new state legislature called for a state convention to examine the national tariff laws. State elections chose delegates, most of whom favored nullification. The convention met and declared both the Tariff of 1828 and the Tariff of 1832 null and void within South Carolina. The convention also passed resolu-tions making it illegal to collect the tariffs within the state. Then, the state legislature approved measures to enforce the nullifica-tion law and strengthened its militia system. South Carolina ap-peared to be preparing for a military showdown with the federal government. To get ready for a possible conflict, South Carolina elected Robert Hayne governor of the state. Then, the legislature selected John C. Calhoun to take Hayne's seat in the U.S. Senate. Calhoun resigned as vice president in December 1832 in order to represent his state in the Senate.

President Jackson was furious at Calhoun's disloyalty. Jackson openly described nullification as treason and all who supported it as traitors to the Union. Then, to ensure the tariffs were collected, the president sent a warship to Charleston Harbor. As soon as Congress assembled in early 1833, Jackson asked for authority to deal with the mounting crisis. Jackson's supporters in Congress submitted a "force bill" giving the president the power to use the Army and Navy to enforce Congressional acts.

In the Senate, Calhoun opposed the force bill. Senator Daniel Webster argued for majority rule, criticizing South Carolina for making the situation worse. As the debate continued, more and more Southern members of Congress spoke out in favor of the force bill. Calhoun realized that his state stood alone against the federal government, but to back down now would end his career. Calhoun was unsure about what to do next, so Henry Clay stepped in to mediate the conflict.

Clay, the former Speaker of the House, was a newly elected senator from the state of Kentucky. Clay put together a compromise whereby the tariff would decrease each year, from 1833 until 1842. In the final year of reductions, the tariff levels would be roughly at the levels of the 1816 tariffs. Congress agreed with Clay, but passed both the compromise and the force bill on the same day. Jackson was content to end the crisis under the terms of the compromise bill.

The compromise allowed Calhoun and South Carolina to back down gracefully. South Carolina, however, was determined to make another statement in defense of its cause. The nullification convention met again and overturned its nullification of the 1828 and 1832 tariffs. Because the compromise had already dealt with the issue of these tariffs, the convention's actions were unnecessary and largely symbolic. The convention was not finished, however. Before closing, the convention nullified the force act. Again, such a resolution was only symbolic, since the force act only applied if South Carolina attempted to interfere with the collection of tariffs.

Calhoun and South Carolina lost the battle over nullification. The senator learned a valuable lesson, however: No state can stand alone against the federal government. In the years that followed, Calhoun championed states' rights and worked to build a strong union of Southern states. His efforts resulted in a defined section of the United States that stood as a unified block in Congress. Thus, the South in 1860 would respond very differently to the questions of states' rights and secession than it had in 1833.

# Manifest Destiny

The presence of slavery in the South and the lack of slavery in the North continued to lead to friction between the two sections. Compromise was relatively painless in the early years, for two key reasons: First, many Americans in both the North and the South wanted to see the new nation grow and survive. Consequently, when the issue of slavery surfaced, such as during the Constitutional Convention in 1787, compromise was a goal desired by both sides. Second, until the Louisiana Purchase doubled the size of the United States, there was a roughly equal opportunity for both sections to experience about the same rate of growth. The Louisiana Purchase in 1803 opened up a completely new region into which the young nation would expand.

It is little surprise that the first major political clash concerning the expansion or limitation of slavery took place when Missouri applied for statehood. Missouri was the northernmost territory from the original Louisiana Purchase to seek admission into the Union. Missouri's location placed it as far north as Ohio, Indiana, and Illinois—three of the five states carved out of the original Northwest Territory, and where Congress had banned slavery. This key fact helps explain why Congress wrestled with admitting Missouri and eventually compromised by establishing the 36° 30' line between slave and free territory for all remaining land from the Louisiana Purchase. Henry Clay and the other leaders meant for the compromise to settle the slave question.

It appears that none of the leaders in 1820, however, foresaw the immense growth in U.S. territory over the next three decades. Unfortunately, the most visionary leaders and thoughtful statesmen failed to imagine the rapid expansion in U.S. territory that would occur before 1850. There may be many reasons for the territorial growth, but the driving force was the vision of Manifest Destiny.

The term *Manifest Destiny* represents a belief that it was the clear fate or destiny of the United States to lay claim to the North American continent. The ideal captured the imagination of the American people in the 1840s, even though the concept of Manifest Destiny had been around for some time. An expansionist editor named John O'Sullivan coined the term in 1845 to explain the values and beliefs of many other Americans who expected their nation to grow. O'Sullivan's term referred to the expected U.S. annexation of Texas, but the term soon encompassed all U.S. expansion. O'Sullivan supported gradual U.S. expansion through settlement. The editor believed that such settlers would naturally take the institutions of U.S. government and society with them and reproduce them wherever they settled. In time, communities and residents in those territories would almost certainly desire to join the United States.

Unfortunately, O'Sullivan did not recognize the power of his words. Others used Manifest Destiny to defend the taking of land from Mexico in the Mexican-American War. Some believed that Manifest Destiny was not merely a possible direction for U.S. policy, but a responsibility. As William Earl Weeks notes, "It appeared to be America's sacred duty to expand across the North American continent, to reign supreme in the Western Hemisphere, and to serve as an example of the future to people everywhere. This was the Manifest Destiny of the American people." Throughout the 1840s, many Americans came to view expansion across the continent as sure to happen.

## THE CHANGING VIEW OF MANIFEST DESTINY

As Southerners sought to expand slavery, some adjusted the purpose of Manifest Destiny to fit their changing vision of the United States. Some viewed territorial expansion as the only way to preserve the Southern way of life. This fits in well with Manifest Destiny. After all, the belief that Americans extended their culture through expansion was a prominent feature of Manifest Destiny. In the 1840s and 1850s, Americans in the South took hold of Manifest Destiny and applied it to their unique culture. Believing they faced growth or decline, many Southerners preferred expansion to maintaining the status quo. As Reginald C. Stuart explains, "Southerners wanted new land because they believed that slavery must expand or else shrivel and die."

Author Albert K. Weinberg explains Southern thinking concerning Texas annexation: "Whereas it had once been feared that the existence of the Union was jeopardized by expansion, it was now apprehended that the Union might be [endangered] by failure to expand through annexing Texas." While many in the North viewed expansion as the source of tension with the South, many of their Southern counterparts held the opposite view. The lack of expansion irritated Southerners who viewed such nonaction as a limitation on their way of life. Weinberg writes, "The Southern States held Texas to be necessary to their economic prosperity, the security of their 'peculiar institution,' and their maintenance of a balance of political power with the North."

Since Northern states banned slavery, the South looked to annexation as the means by which to expand slavery and

*The most famous painting illustrating the idea of Manifest Destiny is "American Progress." In this artwork, a female power, representing the United States, brings progress, education, and technology to the West while pushing out Native Americans and rustic wilderness. This notion of Manifest Destiny caused further friction between the North and South as both sides debated the allowance of slavery in the new western territories.*

grow their national influence. The key to protecting slavery was territorial expansion, which in turn would lead to future slave states sending elected representatives to Washington, D.C. Historian Lars Schoultz quotes a Southern member of Congress who understood the fate of his region if there were no expansion: "Every census has added to the power of the nonslaveholding States, and diminished that of the South. We are growing weaker, and they stronger, every day." The South stood to lose national influence unless more slave states entered the Union. If the North continued to limit the expansion of slavery in the territories, then the South could not expand its power base. Southerners faced a dim political reality: Without expansion, the slaveholding states would continually hold less power in the national government. This fact, perhaps more than any

## Barnburners

In the 1840s, the slavery issue increasingly exposed divisions within the Whigs and Democrats, threatening the unity of each party. The Democrats wrestled among themselves, with a group of reform-minded members opposed to extending slavery in the territories. David Wilmot was one of these reformers within his party. He was the author of the Wilmot Proviso that attempted to limit slavery in any territory the United States might gain in the war with Mexico.

This bloc of Northern Democrats, mostly from New York, opposed the extension of slavery. One of their most prominent supporters was former president Martin Van Buren. Many Democrats viewed this group as radical, fearing that its persistent stands on some of the issues would cost their party votes and elections. Critics called this group the barnburners. The term *barnburner* paints a visual picture of a senseless farmer who burned down his own barn in order to eliminate a plague of rats. Mainstream Democrats feared the barnburners were willing to destroy the party over the slavery issue. Their fears were justified: In 1848, the barnburners joined with abolitionists and antislavery Whigs to form the Free Soil Party in 1848. The Free Soil Party nominated Van Buren as its candidate, splitting the Democrat vote in several key states. The move cost Democrat Lewis Cass the election, handing the presidency to the Whig candidate, Zachary Taylor. The effect of the barnburners demonstrated the explosive nature of the slavery issue and pointed to future divisions in the public over slavery.

other, led many in 1861 to conclude that the South needed to leave the Union.

Historian William Earl Weeks explains that justifying expansion with Manifest Destiny presented a persuasive argument. Weeks observes that under the guidance "of virtue, mission, and destiny evolved a powerful nationalist mythology that was virtually impossible to oppose." Thus, Manifest Destiny became a political weapon, wielded by advocates of expansion. Those advocates wrapped their arguments in a fierce patriotic spirit, often concealing their true intentions. For some, those intentions were nothing less than the acquisition of territory in order to expand slavery. Nowhere were these intentions clearer than in the war with Mexico.

## THE WAR WITH MEXICO AND THE WILMOT PROVISO

In 1846, the United States went to war with Mexico. The war was popular, especially at the beginning. Some people, however, opposed the war from the start. As the conflict continued, others began to criticize the president.

The war was somewhat predictable two years before it began. James Polk had campaigned for president on a promise of expansion, vowing to secure Oregon in the Northwest and settle the Texas question in the Southwest. Texas became an independent republic in 1836 and applied for U.S. statehood. Mexico continued to claim Texas as part of its territory, and the United States seemed unwilling to get involved until admitting Texas as a state in 1845.

Following his inauguration, Polk stationed federal troops in Texas under General Zachary Taylor to protect the Texas border. Mexico and the United States, however, argued over the location of that border. The United States claimed the Rio Grande, while the Mexican government claimed the Nueces River. A brief skirmish within the disputed territory resulted in 11 dead

Americans, after which Polk asked Congress to issue a declaration of war. Congress declared war on Mexico on May 13, 1846.

On August 8, 1846, Polk asked Congress for $2 million to finance costs associated with the treaty negotiations with Mexico. The war had only begun three months earlier, so the request for appropriations to conclude the war was premature. The conflict was still raging, and Mexico showed no signs of giving in. Indeed, Mexico had repeatedly vowed to continue fighting. At best, Polk's request was rushing to judgment. At worst, the spending request was thoughtless. Congressional opponents used the bill as an opportunity to begin a discussion on what the United States might gain in the war.

Some in Congress wanted to resist the president and the spending bill gave them the perfect opportunity to challenge the idea that the United States should gain more territory from the conflict. Resistance to Polk's war aims came from an unlikely source: a Northern Democrat. David Wilmot, a Pennsylvania representative, was serving his first term in the House. In August 1846, while Congress debated Polk's budget requests for the war, Wilmot introduced an amendment, later called the Wilmot Proviso. His resolution stated:

> Provided, That, as an express and fundamental condition to the acquisition of any territory from the Republic of Mexico by the United States, by virtue of any treaty which may be negotiated between them, and to the use by the Executive of the moneys herein appropriated, neither slavery nor involuntary servitude shall ever exist in any part of said territory, except for crime, whereof the party shall first be duly convicted.

The proviso did not specifically oppose the war, but it did propose to limit slavery in any territory the United States gained through the war. Since Polk and many supporters of the war viewed the conflict as an opportunity to expand U.S. territory, the proviso was a direct assault on their war aims. The Wilmot

Proviso did not seek to limit slavery where it existed, but it did recommend limiting the expansion of slavery.

Although brief, Wilmot's amendment provoked strong reactions from supporters and opponents alike. Those opposing the amendment offered a plan whereby the Missouri Compromise line would extend to the Pacific Coast. That proposal failed, forcing the House to vote on the Wilmot Proviso. The House approved the measure as part of the spending bill. Opponents tried to kill the bill, but in the end, the House sent the bill—with Wilmot's amendment intact—to the Senate.

The House votes revealed the passions on the subject. Many Southerners believed the provision was an attempt to deny them their constitutional property rights, which would include slaves, considering the proposal as proof of Northern conspiracies to end slavery. Some within the South judged the measure to come from Northern pride and a bias against Southern culture and society. This turned many Southerners against Wilmot and his proviso. Historian William W. Freehling believes that "most Southerners raged primarily because David Wilmot's holier-than-thou stance was so insulting." The voting record on Wilmot's Proviso supports Freehling's argument. A representative's party membership was less important than his home state. Votes on the Wilmot Proviso pointed to a growing separation between the North and South.

The Senate failed to ratify the spending bill, including the Wilmot Proviso. The president, however, reignited the argument when he again asked Congress for end-of-the-war negotiations money in his annual message to Congress. This time, Polk asked for $3 million, and he offered some rationale for seizing the territory from Mexico. The president explained that the United States had not gone to war in order to acquire territory. Instead, the nation had simply fought to defend and maintain its boundary. Nonetheless, any respectable peace settlement had to include some compensation to the winner of the war, the United States. The Mexican economy was poor, so the only possible compensation was territory.

When the House considered this spending request, the antislavery seeds planted by Wilmot began to grow. Another Northerner, Preston King of New York, offered his own amendment that expanded the Wilmot Proviso. King's amendment extended restrictions on slavery to any territory the United States might gain in the future—not just the territory it expected to receive from Mexico.

In the end, King's measure, like Wilmot's, failed to pass, though the ideals of the Wilmot Proviso persisted. The same kind of restrictions resurfaced when the Senate considered ratifying the final treaty with Mexico. The Democrats soon came up with their own approach for dealing with slavery in the territories: popular sovereignty. In simple terms, popular sovereignty means that an issue is decided by popular vote. That is, let the people decide the issue.

The Wilmot Proviso began a national debate that continued until Southern states left the Union and civil war broke out. The philosophy of Manifest Destiny, which called on Americans to fulfill their destiny and claim western lands, propelled slavery into the national debate. That philosophy drove the United States to continue to seek more territory, even though additional territory led to arguments over slavery.

## THE COMPROMISE OF 1850

In 1850, there were at least five major issues facing the national government, four of which were extremely controversial. The issues all dealt with western territories or slavery or both. The war with Mexico had led to troubling times in U.S. politics. Under the terms of the peace treaty, the United States gained a large territory from Mexico. Now, the question that had plagued the nation since its founding resurfaced once again: Should there be restrictions on slavery in the territory? The bulk of the American Southwest remained unsettled, including what later became New Mexico, Arizona, Utah, and Nevada. Many wanted to see that land organized into territories. The process for territorial organization, however, led to questions of whether to permit slavery. A further complication involved Texas land claims to land north and west of the Texas Panhandle. The federal government could not organize any territories out of the land until settling the dispute with Texas.

In the case of California, the discovery of gold near Sacramento in 1848 led to a massive influx of settlers the following year. Although most of the settlers did not find their fortune in gold, many did decide to stay in California. These recently arrived residents wanted California to enter the Union as a free state. Since the Senate at the time contained an equal number of slave states and free states, Southerners opposed this proposal.

The South was also unhappy over ways in which Northern abolitionists and local officials undermined the federal fugitive slave laws. The question of slavery in Washington, D.C., also played a role in the political dialogue. Northerners found it repulsive that slavery was legal in the nation's capital. Worse yet, the capital city boasted a large and profitable slave market. Within view of Capitol Hill, slaves were bought and sold in the same manner as livestock. Increasingly, Northerners found the practice too much to stomach. Lawmakers from Northern states proposed banning the slave trade and slavery in Washington, D.C.

Henry Clay attempted to forge a compromise, presenting his ideas for a deal in January 1850. Now a senator from the state of Kentucky, the 70-year-old worked with Daniel Webster and Stephen A. Douglas for six months to reach a settlement. Clay took the same approach that had worked 30 years earlier— placing all of the pieces of the compromise within one large bill. This time, however, the strategy failed to work. Clay found it impossible to get a majority to support the bill. His ideas also triggered strong reactions against several of the bill's proposals.

One strong voice of opposition was that of South Carolina senator John C. Calhoun. The defender of states' rights believed the compromise would further weaken the ability of the South to defend itself from attempts to limit slavery in Southern states. During the debates, Calhoun was ill and dying, but he still wrote a speech and sat in the Senate chamber while a colleague read it on the Senate floor. Calhoun argued that the North needed to give the South equal power in the national government in order to save the Union. Calhoun wanted an amendment to the Constitution that ensured a balance of power between the sections. The South Carolina senator did not want a short-term compromise but a long-term solution to the problems of division between the two regions. The speech failed to convince the Senate that the North needed to listen to the minority rights of the South. A few weeks after the speech, John C. Calhoun died.

Clay and others labored for six months, but the measure failed to pass in the Senate, as many Northerners and Southerners voted against it. In some respects, the effort appeared meaningless since President Taylor had pledged to veto the bill. Instead, Taylor wished for the territories of California, Minnesota, New Mexico, Oregon, and Utah to enter the Union with no requirements regarding slavery. Because each of the territories prohibited slavery, Taylor's leadership would have given the North a five-state majority (or 10 more seats) in the Senate to go along with its majority in the House. The chance for compromise appeared to be gone.

Suddenly, Zachary Taylor died on July 9, 1850, and was succeeded by Vice President Millard Fillmore, who supported compromise. Stephen A. Douglas of Illinois stepped into the leadership role to forge an agreement. Douglas understood that different sections of the country opposed different parts of the compromise. Since Douglas believed in the legislation, he took a different approach than the one Clay followed. First, he broke the bill into five separate bills. As a result, Douglas could then build a different base of support for each bill. Most of the provisions in the five bills came directly from the original proposal. The following is how the final bills dealt with each issue.

Texas still owed Mexico money for various claims dating back to the 1830s. To settle the land dispute, Texas gave up its claims to disputed territory, and in exchange, the U.S. government paid $10 million to cover the Texan debt to Mexico. With secure title to western lands now in place, the United States organized the territories of New Mexico, Arizona, Utah, and Nevada. However, the compromise did not even mention slavery in the new territories. Instead, popular sovereignty would decide the fate of slavery in the four new territories.

The compromise also banned the slave trade in Washington, D.C., although slavery was still legal there. California would be admitted as a free state. A new, tougher Fugitive Slave Act was also included. This law obliged citizens to help slave owners recover fugitive slaves. Requirements were lowered on slave owners wishing to file a claim. To handle the cases, the law created commissioners who received $5 for each alleged fugitive released, but $10 for each alleged fugitive returned. Provisions of this law specified that fugitives had no right to a trial by jury, since a commissioner decided each case. Finally, under this legislation, the government was to hire more federal officials to enforce the law.

Blacks living in the North felt the effects of the law immediately. Many former slaves fled to Canada to avoid being sent back to the South. Dishonest bounty hunters and commissioners wrongfully seized free blacks and placed them in slavery. Lacking the protection of federal courts, free blacks had little choice other than to submit to the law or flee the United States. The Fugitive Slave Act also emboldened abolitionists, who increased efforts to end slavery. The decade prior to the Civil War was the height of the Underground Railroad and other activist efforts to help escaped slaves. The enforcement of the law also helped change the attitudes of many Northerners to be against slavery.

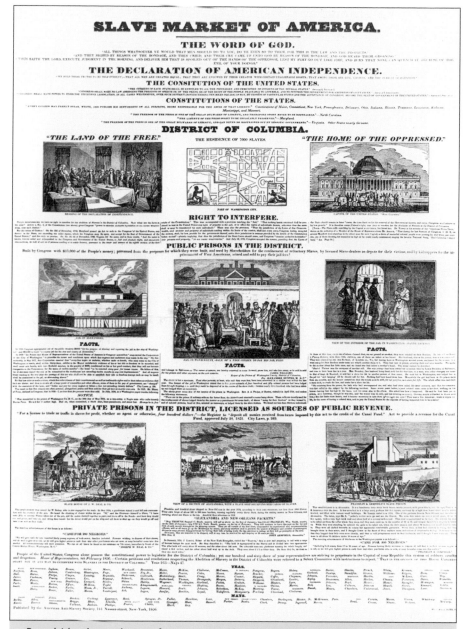

Broadsides, large sheets of paper conveying messages, were the preferred method of distributing a group's views and goals to the public. When the issue of ending slavery in Washington, D.C., arose in the federal government, abolitionists created this broadside in an effort to gain public support for their cause.

Legislators intended that the five laws would balance the interests of slave states and free states. Unfortunately, the Compromise of 1850 was a compromise in name only. Neither section supported objectionable parts of the legislation. Indeed, political realities forced Douglas to break the bill apart in order to secure passage of each provision, demonstrating the inflexibility of each side in the debate. Worse still, the compromise did not end the slavery debate. Northern activists vigorously opposed the new Fugitive Slave Act, while slave owners resented the end of the slave trade in Washington, D.C.

In the end, there were only 4 senators and 28 members of the House who supported each of the five measures. Therefore, despite the passage of each portion of the compromise, there was very little support for the overall compromise. The series of laws gave the impression of compromise, but neither section had compromised with the other. As a substitute for compromise, each section supported the bills they found favorable, while allowing the other section to pass their bills, too. Were it not for Douglas's political moves, neither side could even claim victory for the bills they did support.

President Fillmore signed each of the five bills. The Compromise of 1850 was now the law of the land. In many respects, the compromise failed to accomplish the unity for which Clay had hoped. In the end, the bargain only delayed the breakup of the Union. Instead of ending the slavery issue, the compromise raised slavery to the centerpiece issue for the next decade. The 1850s proved to be a rough decade, with regional tensions rising over the question of slavery. Whereas the Missouri Compromise had satisfied both sections, few Americans were content with anything in the 1850 agreement. The so-called compromise only temporarily concealed the divisions stemming from slavery. As an alternative to genuine cooperation, the Compromise of 1850 drove the two sections apart. Further, the agreement revealed how the issue of slavery divided the nation.

# Bleeding Kansas

In 1854, Illinois senator Stephen Douglas submitted a controversial bill that disrupted the entire political establishment. The effects of his proposal included the death of the Whig Party and the birth of a new party, the Republicans. The bill also put Douglas's own party at risk, threatening to divide the Democrats along sectional lines. The completed piece of legislation was the Kansas-Nebraska Act of 1854.

Stephen Douglas was a man of the West. Born in Vermont, Douglas went to Illinois at age 20 and made his career there, first as a lawyer, then as a politician. What he lacked in physical height, Douglas made up for in intellect, determination, and his fiery speaking ability. Standing just 5-feet-4-inches tall, friends and foes alike called him "the Little Giant." As a senator, Douglas chaired the important Committee on Territories. Douglas and others wanted to encourage settlement across the plains, which would aid efforts to construct a transcontinental railroad through the region.

## THE KANSAS-NEBRASKA ACT OF 1854

The Kansas-Nebraska Act established two territories, Kansas and Nebraska, out of western land on the Great Plains. The act also overturned the Missouri Compromise, allowing settlers of each territory to determine the legal status of slavery. When President Pierce signed the act into law, many in the North

# Whig Presidents

After Congress enacted the Kansas-Nebraska Act of 1854, the Whig Party fell apart. Antislavery Whigs splintered the party. The national structure never recovered. The Whigs nominated presidential candidates in 1856 and 1860, but lacked a national organization. As a political force, the Whigs were no longer competitive in national politics after 1854.

The Whig Party had come into existence in 1833 to 1834, during the second presidential term of Andrew Jackson. In many respects, the party was a redecorated version of the Federalist Party, which had died out after the presidential elections of 1816. The number one issue uniting most Whigs in the mid-1830s was a strong dislike and distrust of Andrew Jackson. The Whigs soon advocated a strong nationalist economic policy, led by Henry Clay and Daniel Webster.

In presidential elections, the Whigs were largely unsuccessful. In its 20 or so years of existence, the Whig Party only won the presidency in 1840 and 1848. Both times, its candidate was a war hero. In 1840, William Henry Harrison won, but died a month after taking office. His vice president, John Tyler, a former Democrat-Republican, took over for him. Tyler was from Virginia and strongly supported states' rights, which put him at odds with the Whig members of Congress. After Tyler vetoed virtually the entire Whig legislative plan, the Whigs kicked him out of the party. Tyler spent openly opposed it. Many, however, decided to do more than complain in political newspapers. Instead, passage of the act spurred many to action. Citizens, activists, and politicians, all unhappy at the ineffectiveness of the Whigs and the direction of the Democrats, began seeking other ways to promote their cause. The result was the founding of a new political party.

the rest of his presidency working more closely with the Democrats than with his own former party.

The second Whig president was Zachary Taylor, a career soldier from Louisiana who had never before held an elected office. Taylor owned slaves, but opposed the extension of slavery into the territories. Taylor supported Whig policies, declaring his opposition to the Compromise of 1850. Henry Clay, although a Whig, desperately wanted to pass the compromise, but failed to gain the necessary votes. Taylor died unexpectedly in 1850, and Vice President Millard Fillmore succeeded him.

President Fillmore presided over the decline of the Whigs. Unlike Taylor, the New York native supported the Compromise of 1850, signing each of the separate bills into law. Fillmore's signature on the Fugitive Slave Act caused many within his own party to reject his leadership. In 1852, Fillmore had lost so much support that he could not even win the presidential nomination. Instead, the Whigs selected another war hero, Winfield Scott. This time, however, the party needed something more appealing than a former general to head its ticket. Scott lost, and the Whig Party quickly fell.

The legacy of the Whig presidents is one of lost opportunities. Both Whig presidents died in office. Both of their vice presidents, after becoming the chief executive, supported policies that went against the Whig platform. Thus, the Whigs never accomplished their goals of a national economic policy. In the aftermath of the Whigs' collapse, a new party would emerge that would later enact many of the early Whig dreams of government-supported improvements to education and sound monetary policies.

Most opposition to the Kansas-Nebraska Act concerned popular sovereignty. Some were angry with Douglas for reopening old wounds by effectively overturning the Missouri Compromise. Others feared that the act did more than allow settlers to choose. After all, the act created two territories divided along an east-west boundary, meaning there was a Northern and a Southern territory. Because the issue of slavery was divided between the North and South, many concluded this was another action to appease the slaveholding South.

In 1846, David Wilmot had thrown the issue of slavery into the western territories, resulting in a deepening divide between the North and South. The Kansas-Nebraska Act of 1854 managed to inflict still more wounds on the relationship between the two sections. Still, the bill's author, Stephen Douglas, believed he had a solution to the problem. The act itself divided the unorganized territory west of Iowa and Missouri into two separate territories. The 40th parallel served as the dividing line. South of the line was the Kansas Territory. The Nebraska Territory lay north of the line. The two new territories were part of the original Louisiana Purchase. Thus, both Kansas and Nebraska fell under the requirements of the Missouri Compromise, which restricted slavery north of the 36° 30' line. In short, the Kansas-Nebraska Act reopened the slavery issue in territories where many believed the issue had been settled in 1820.

Douglas adapted a term and idea that some within his party had expressed in the past. The Illinois senator put forward the idea of popular sovereignty. Since slavery was the hot-button issue that concerned many leaders in Washington, Douglas proposed transferring the burden of deciding the issue to the residents of territories. To Douglas, the rule of the people should carry more weight than Congress on an issue that affected the local society. Douglas believed that the residents of a territory should determine whether they wanted slavery. In many respects, this was a compromise position. On one side, supporters of slavery demanded that present and future territories include legal safeguards for slavery. On the other side, antislavery supporters insisted that territories bar slavery. Popular sovereignty offered an alternative that gave hope to both sides. Unfortunately, neither side was in the mood to compromise with the other.

To the Little Giant, the issue of slavery was a non-issue. Douglas personally did not care for slavery, but his opposition did not stem from moral objections. Rather, Douglas believed that slavery did not make economic sense. In his travels across the country, he had observed that individuals and communities in free territories were more vibrant, more energetic, and more prosperous than in places where slavery was legal. Douglas firmly believed that if citizens were given the choice, they would choose to limit slavery.

Activists on both sides quickly turned the Kansas situation into a political one. Most of the Missouri slave owners had few slaves. The owners made up a small proportion of the state population. Slavery, however, was indeed a part of Missouri culture and society. In addition, Missouri was already bordered by two other free states, Illinois to the east and Iowa to the north. If Kansas prohibited slavery, then Missouri would sit next to three free states. Many Missouri slave owners feared abolitionist activity. Because slave owners viewed runaway slaves as a financial loss, few were pleased at the prospect of another potential haven for escaped slaves.

Each application for statehood offered the potential for a crisis, as had been the case with California in 1850. The Senate, which continued to hold the promise to Southerners for an approximate equality in power, was shaky at best. Settlers populating western territories wanted to become part of the United States.

The question was one of timing. At what point was the legality of slavery decided: When the territory was organized, or at the time of statehood? The issue was particularly thorny for Democrats, since Northerners and Southerners within the

*Stephen Douglas's original intent in creating the Kansas-Nebraska Act was to acquire territory to help him establish a transcontinental railway from Chicago to the West Coast. By introducing this bill to Congress, Douglas created a firestorm of controversy because the act repealed the Missouri Compromise and established popular sovereignty, which bolstered states' rights regarding slavery.*

party could not agree among themselves. Northern Democrats favored establishing the standard from the start, at the time Congress organized each territory. Southerners disagreed, believing the territory's residents should decide when ratifying the proposed state constitution, thereby increasing the amount of time in which slavery might be established within an area.

Douglas, however, knew he needed Southern votes to win passage of the bill. He reopened the possibility of slavery in the territories by allowing the territories to decide the matter for themselves. Douglas and other supporters of the bill were unprepared for the intense reaction of the North. While Southerners rejoiced, Northerners expressed anger over the legislation.

Douglas knew how to secure a victory in the matter, and earned the backing of the president. Because Pierce was of the Democrat Party, the move placed Northern Democrats in the delicate position of pleasing those who elected them or pleasing their president. The bill passed both houses, and President Pierce signed the Kansas-Nebraska Act into law.

The Kansas-Nebraska Act of 1854 upset the shaky political balance that had existed in Washington since the Missouri Compromise. Besides creating two separate territories, a Northern one and a Southern one, the act also reversed what the 1820 compromise had established nearly 35 years earlier. Under the new law, the federal government no longer banned slavery in the region. In its place, either territory could enter the Union as slave or free, to be determined at the time the territory applied for admission.

The Kansas-Nebraska Act did more than just cause almost immediate political turmoil. The act also led to some of the most bizarre events of the period. Soon, the nation faced violence in Kansas, a shake-up in the two-party system, and an attack on the floor of the Senate, and all of it stemmed from the issue of slavery in the territories.

Soon, a court case further threatened to divide the nation over the slavery issue. Like Douglas, the justices of the Supreme

Court believed their ruling would end the debate over slavery in the territories. Like Douglas, the Supreme Court misjudged the situation. As a result, the slavery issue continued to escalate tensions and pointed to something far worse than strong disagreements: civil war. Nowhere was the growing divide between the North and the South clearer than in Kansas. Events there strengthened both sections, increasing tensions and the influence of radical voices, especially in the South.

## BLEEDING KANSAS

Northern anger now turned to rage. Most believed that there would be no attempts to take slaves into Nebraska, due to its location and climate. Kansas, however, was another matter. Many believed eastern Kansas, with its climate and nearness to slavery in western Missouri, might be ideal for slavery. Congressman Eli Thayer of New York and other leaders organized the New England Emigrant Aid Company. This organization intended to help antislavery settlers move to Kansas in order to ensure it remained a free territory.

A year after the Kansas-Nebraska Act became law, 1,200 antislavery settlers from northeastern states had already arrived in Kansas. At least 800 others made their way westward in the coming months. Henry Ward Beecher, a prominent Northern clergyman, raised money to arm antislavery settlers with Sharps rifles, which some then called "Beecher's Bibles." Distorted stories in the press made it appear that abolitionists were populating Kansas as part of some Yankee conspiracy. False reports in the South warned of 20,000 Northern abolitionists flooding into Kansas. Despite the fears and rumors, the largest influx of settlers into Kansas actually came from Missouri.

When the Kansas Territory held elections in November 1854 to choose its representative to Washington, 1,700 armed Missourians crossed the border and voted in Kansas. As the Missourians had hoped, their ballots helped select a pro-slavery

delegate. In order to choose members of the territorial legislature, another election was held in March 1855. Once again,
thousands of Missourians (called Border Ruffians) streamed
across the border to cast illegal votes. Voter registration rolls
contained fewer than 3,000 registered voters; however, more
than 6,300 voted for the pro-slavery candidates. Fewer than
800 voted against slavery. Pro-slavery forces from Missouri had
hijacked the electoral process, which was supposed to ensure
popular sovereignty. Congress investigated the election, finding
that nearly 5,000 votes were frauds. The presence, however, of
so many armed Missourians just across the border unsettled
the territorial governor, who decided not to call for another
election.

The new territorial legislature wasted no time in enacting
a slave code. These laws did more than just allow slavery. They
also included punishments to silence the opposition. Only men
acknowledged as pro-slavery could hold office in the territorial government. Any person speaking out against slavery faced
imprisonment. Death was the possible sentence for anyone
who spoke or wrote in favor of a slave rebellion or helped fugitive slaves. The territorial government of Kansas was decidedly
pro-slavery.

Free-state settlers decided to take action, gathering in Lawrence and organizing themselves into a free-state party. This
group held an election to select delegates to draft a territo-
rial/state constitution, an election which the pro-slavery forces
boycotted. After drafting a free-state constitution, the free-state
legislature met in Topeka during the winter of 1855 to 1856.
Despite stories told in the press, this group was unquestionably
in the free-state camp, voting to ban all blacks from Kansas.

Kansas, as a divided territory, symbolized the divisions
within the United States. Historian James M. McPherson, in his
book *Ordeal by Fire: The Civil War and Reconstruction*, writes,
"Kansas now had two territorial governments—one legal but
fraudulent, the other illegal but representing a majority of the

settlers." Worse yet, different leaders in Washington recognized different legislatures. The Republicans, who dominated the House of Representatives, acknowledged the free-state legislature, while Pierce and the Democrat-controlled Senate recognized the pro-slavery body as legitimate.

In 1856, the pro-slavery force moved its capital to Lecompton, located just 12 miles (19 km) from the free-state center of Lawrence. That same year, a congressional committee arrived in Kansas to investigate the previous elections. The committee determined that widespread fraud had taken place. The Pierce administration and leading Democrats refused to recognize the free-state legislature, however. Instead, the U.S. government viewed the pro-slavery legislature as the legitimate leadership in Kansas.

In the spring of 1856, tensions reached a breaking point when pro-slavery forces attacked free-state settlers in Lawrence. The pro-slavery force destroyed two printing presses, plundered businesses and homes, and set fire to the Free State Hotel. Free-state radicals, led by John Brown and four of his sons, hit back in gruesome fashion. At Pottawatomie Creek, Brown and his band of men captured five pro-slavery men and killed them with swords.

In September 1856, John W. Geary, the third governor of the territory, arrived in Kansas and established order. Geary had already served as the first mayor of San Francisco and would later serve as a Union general during the Civil War and two terms as Pennsylvania governor following the war. The bleeding in Kansas ended, but about 55 people had paid with their lives in the violence. There were various attempts made by both sides to draft a Kansas constitution to allow the territory to apply for statehood. The final constitution, which was free-state, was the work of a convention in Wyandotte. Kansas sent this constitution to Washington to gain entry into the Union, but Southern states blocked its admittance. The chaos in the territory and political play prevented Kansas from becoming a state

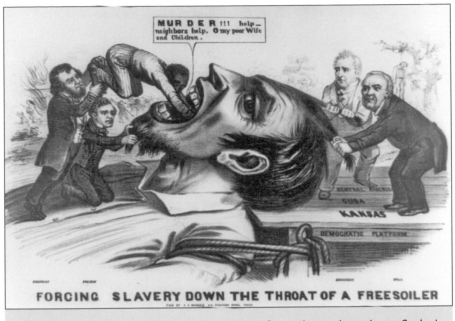

FORCING SLAVERY DOWN THE THROAT OF A FREESOILER

*After establishing popular sovereignty in Kansas, free-soilers and pro-slavers flocked to the new territory, hoping to vote and sway the poll in their favor. The two sides lived in close proximity until a group of pro-slavers violently attacked a group of antislavery settlers in Lawrence, Kansas. That incident began a murderous back-and-forth exchange of retaliation. Above, a political cartoon blames pro-slavery advocates for trying to force the issue of slavery upon free-soilers.*

until January 1861. Kansas won its statehood, entering as a free state, but only because several Southern states had seceded and withdrawn their representatives from Washington.

## THE CANING OF SUMNER

While events in Kansas spiraled out of control, the political situation in Washington also became strained. On May 19 and 20, Massachusetts senator Charles Sumner addressed the situation in Kansas. Speaking in the Senate Chamber, Sumner entitled his remarks "The Crime Against Kansas." First, Sumner condemned the Kansas-Nebraska Act and its authors, Andrew Butler of South Carolina and Stephen Douglas. Historian Alan

Brinkley records how the Massachusetts senator used a sexual slur when discussing Butler, accusing the Southerner of having taken "a mistress . . . who, though ugly to others, is always lovely to him; though polluted in the sight of the world, is chaste in his sight . . . the harlot, slavery." Sumner also made fun of Butler's speech troubles and some of his physical movements, both the lingering results of a stroke.

Two days later, South Carolina congressman Preston Brooks entered the nearly empty Senate Chamber and approached Sumner, who was seated at his desk. According to historian James M. McPherson, Brooks told Sumner that his speech was "a libel on South Carolina and Mr. Butler, who is a relative of mine." Sumner started to stand, but Brooks began to beat him on the head with a cane. Sumner found his legs pinned under the desk, which was bolted to the floor. With Sumner unable to escape, Brooks repeatedly struck the senator with his cane, landing 30 or more blows on the poor man. Brooks continued hitting Sumner even after he broke his cane over the senator's head. Finally, the bleeding Sumner managed to pull the desk loose before collapsing on the floor. Others entered the room and prevented Brooks from continuing the attack.

The caning of Sumner brought forth vastly different responses from different parts of the country. In the South, Brooks was an instant hero. Admirers from across the South sent him new canes as congratulations. The House punished Brooks, but Southern votes prevented the two-thirds majority needed to remove him. Brooks resigned, but his home district immediately and overwhelmingly reelected him, whereupon he retook his seat in the House.

The attack left Sumner a wounded man. He did not attend the Senate for more than three years, seeking help from various doctors and treatments. Massachusetts reelected him to the Senate, allowing his seat to remain vacant. His unfilled chair served as a strong reminder of the attack on Sumner.

Northern activists spoke out in favor of free speech and criticized Southern intolerance. William Cullen Bryant, editor of the *New York Evening Post*, challenged such Southern fanaticism:

> Has it come to this, that we must speak with bated breath in the presence of our Southern masters; that even their follies are too sacred a subject to ridicule; that we must not deny the consistency of their principles or the accuracy of their statements? If we venture to laugh at them or question their logic, are we to be chastised as they chastise their slaves? Are we too, slaves, slaves for life, a target for their brutal blows, when we do not comport ourselves to please them?

Many in the North agreed with Bryant. The Republicans responded to the attack by rising to defy Southern bravado. As a result, the Republicans became the alternative to the Democrats, who increasingly found it more difficult to win elections in the North. After the caning of Sumner, the Republicans became a key force in U.S. politics.

# Dred Scott and John Brown

I n the midst of Bleeding Kansas, Americans prepared to elect a president. Incumbent president Franklin Pierce had little backing in the North, due to his support for the Kansas-Nebraska Act, which he signed into law in 1854. The Democrats knew Pierce had no chance of winning the election and did not nominate him in 1856. Instead, the Democrats chose James Buchanan, the American minister to England. Buchanan seemed a safe choice, since he had been out of the country during the Kansas-Nebraska Act, making him the highest-profiled U.S. politician with virtually no stated view on the controversial legislation. Buchanan did not want to run for president, but reluctantly accepted the nomination.

Meanwhile, the newly formed Republican Party nominated John C. Frémont, who had gained fame for his exploits in California during the Mexican-American War. The American Party, also known as the Know Nothings, nominated former president Millard Fillmore. It is likely that Fillmore's presence in the race took votes away from Frémont. Regardless of the reasons, Buchanan won the election and prepared to take office. Awaiting the new president was a highly anticipated Supreme Court ruling involving slavery in the territories. Buchanan was a Washington insider and had heard enough about the ruling before his inauguration to anticipate the Court's decision. Thus, as recorded by historian Don E. Fehrenbacher, the new president

## The Know Nothings

Democrat James Buchanan's 1856 presidential victory over Republican John C. Frémont was largely due to the presence of the Know Nothing Party candidate in the election. Former president Millard Fillmore ran on an antislavery platform, winning enough votes in a few key Northern states to allow Buchanan to win the election with more of the popular vote. Exactly who were the Know Nothings?

The movement began with the formation of the American Republican Party in 1843 in New York. This group was fearful of the large numbers of immigrants flooding into the North and wanted to do something about it. Many within the movement also opposed slavery. Later, the party changed its name to the Native American Party in 1845, and the American Party in 1855. The party was secretive and members were supposed to respond to any questions about party activities with "I know nothing." As a result, most knew the party as the Know Nothings. The party supported strict limits on immigration and gaining U.S. citizenship.

The slavery issue convinced many Know Nothings to join the Republican Party, leading to the demise of the American Party. After the election of 1856, support for the Know Nothings plunged as the Republicans offered the best chance to unite the North against the slave interests of the South. A pro-slavery group within the Know Nothing Party remained active in limited pockets throughout the South, but the party was no longer capable of mounting a serious national campaign.

in his inaugural address on March 4, 1857, said of the expected decision, "To their decision, in common with all good citizens, I shall cheerfully submit, whatever this may be." Unfortunately, few in the North appeared willing to submit to the ruling.

## DRED SCOTT

The court case Buchanan mentioned was *Dred Scott v. Sandford*. The case involved Dred Scott, a slave who had lived for two years in a free territory. Dr. John Emerson, Scott's owner, was a surgeon in the U.S. Army. Emerson's orders took him to Illinois, which was a free state. Emerson took Scott with him. Later, Scott also accompanied Emerson to present-day Minnesota, where slavery was also prohibited under the provisions of the Missouri Compromise. Finally, Emerson took Scott to St. Louis, Missouri, in 1837. Emerson died in 1843 and left Scott to his wife, Irene Emerson, who remarried to an abolitionist. In 1846, Scott filed a lawsuit, arguing that since his owner had taken him to both a free state and free territory, he had become legally free. The case was intended to serve as a test case to help define constitutional law on the status of slavery in the territories.

Scott lost the first legal round when the court ruled that he could not prove he was a slave. The judge ordered a second trial, however, which Irene Emerson appealed. The Missouri State Supreme Court denied her appeal, and the new trial began in January 1850. In this trial, a jury agreed with Scott, declaring him and his family to be legally free. Hearing the appeal, the Missouri State Supreme Court overturned the lower court's ruling in 1852. Scott's owner, however, had since moved to New York, so Scott sued in federal court, since the Constitution allows citizens of one state to sue a citizen of another state in federal court. In 1854, the federal court ruled against Scott, who then appealed to the U.S. Supreme Court, which first heard the case in the spring of 1856.

The nation's high court recognized the political impacts of the case. Thus, the Court listened to arguments again in the 1856-to-1857 term. The longer the case dragged on, the more important it became. After more than 10 years in the courts, the U.S. Supreme Court was finally going to rule on the case. Yet, the politics of slavery had changed since Scott had first filed suit in 1846. In many respects, the case went well beyond the issue of Scott's freedom. Instead, the case provided the court the opportunity to settle the issue of slavery and a government's authority to regulate it. Members of the high court believed their ruling would finally resolve the issue.

## THE *DRED SCOTT* DECISION

The Supreme Court in 1857 was made up of five Southerners and four Northerners. Seven of the justices, including the five Southerners, were Democrats, the very party committed to protecting slavery. Chief Justice Roger B. Taney was a fiery supporter of states' rights. Andrew Jackson had appointed Taney to the Court in 1833 to replace John Marshall, the chief justice who advocated a strong nationalism in his rulings. Until the *Dred Scott* ruling, Taney had established himself as a top judge. Contemporary legal experts respected his reasoning and support of state power. Under normal circumstances and in ordinary times, Taney would deserve consideration as one of the great Supreme Court justices. *Dred Scott v. Sandford,* however, was no ordinary case and 1857 was no ordinary time. Taney's role in the case forever tarnished his reputation.

Essentially, there were three questions facing the Court: First, did Scott's extended stay in a free state or territory make him free? Second, did Scott, as a slave and a black man, have the right to file a suit in a federal court? Third, was the 1820 Missouri Compromise, which had prohibited slavery in the territory where Scott had resided for an extended time,

*Dred Scott, a slave who had worked and lived in two free states with his family and owners, sued for his freedom after he was denied from legally purchasing it. The landmark case* Scott v. Sandford *reached the U.S. Supreme Court, where the justices ruled that Scott could not sue because the U.S. Constitution classified him as property, not as a citizen. This decision further exacerbated tensions between the North and the South.*

constitutional or unconstitutional? The Court easily answered the first question, as previous court decisions had clearly stated that temporary residence in a free state or territory did not grant free status. Consequently, the Court ruled that

Scott was still a slave. The Court could have stopped there by merely upholding the ruling of the federal court—but it did not.

The Court voted and decided to issue its decision upholding the lower court's decision. Historians believe that the Southern members of the Court decided that the case would serve to resolve the slavery issue. "The temptation to settle the vexed territorial question" was simply too strong a temptation for the Court, explains historian James M. McPherson. Rather than simply upholding the previous decision, the justices decided to confront the larger issues. Thus, the uproar over Kansas continued and two days after Buchanan's inauguration, the U.S. Supreme Court handed down a ruling that served to further drive a wedge between the two sections.

Taney wrote what many considered as the opinion of the Court. In reality, the official ruling was somewhat difficult to determine, since each member of the Court wrote his own opinion in the case. (Taney's opinion can be viewed online at supreme.justia.com.) First, the chief justice tackled the issues of Scott's legal status, ruling that Scott was still a slave, regardless of where his master had taken him. Second, Taney claimed that Scott was not a citizen and never could be because he was black. Taney argued that it made no difference if a black person was free or a slave; blacks could not be citizens of any state.

The chief justice also discussed how he believed the Founding Fathers viewed blacks. Taney wrote that blacks had "for more than a century before been regarded as beings of an inferior order, and altogether unfit to associate with the white race, either in social or political relations, and so far inferior that they had no rights which the white man was bound to respect." Finally, Taney argued that the Constitution did not grant Congress the authority to restrict slavery in the federal territories. Under this reasoning, he declared the Missouri Compromise unconstitutional, because Congress lacked the authority to limit slavery in the territories.

The South praised the ruling. Northern Democrats also rejoiced that their views on slavery were now the constitutional interpretation of the Supreme Court. Nevertheless, the vote was split 5 to 4, which provided important political cover for Republicans. Only Southerners and those justices with ties to slave interests had voted for the majority. More important, Justice Benjamin Curtis, who voted against the decision, wrote a stinging dissenting opinion in which he attacked every key point of Chief Justice Taney's majority opinion. Antislavery activists viewed the *Scott* ruling as illegitimate. Ironically, it was now Democrats arguing for national supremacy and the authority of the federal government, as displayed through the Supreme Court.

Taney's harsh words only served to enrage those who disagreed with the Court's decision. Antislavery activists claimed the Court overstepped its authority in the decision. Regardless of the political hazards, Republicans argued against the ruling. Using the Curtis opinion, Republicans pointed out that Taney's ruling went well beyond the facts of the case. The Republicans also charged that slave interests, including those of incoming president Buchanan, had unfairly influenced the justices.

Indeed, Buchanan had sought to influence the Court. The president-elect overstepped acceptable practice when he put pressure on Justice Robert Grier. Party officials and Court insiders knew the outcome of the decision, but wanted to have at least one Northerner with no Southern ties to vote with the majority. Buchanan used his position and influence to persuade Grier to vote with the majority in order to help preserve national unity.

Despite the intentions of the justices, the *Dred Scott* case did not end the slavery question. Instead, the decision worsened the bitterness and divisions between the North and the South. Moreover, Taney's decision did not destroy the Republican Party, but served to back up Republican charges that Southerners were plotting to make slavery legal throughout the entire

# Dred Scott

The U.S. Supreme Court finally ruled on Dred Scott's celebrated case in 1857. Unfortunately, the Court ruled that Scott was still a slave and even denied that he or any black man could be a citizen. The ruling further showed the differences between the North and the South, differences that eventually ended in civil war.

As for Dred Scott, his situation changed, not on constitutional grounds, but due to the goodwill of white abolitionists. After losing his 11-year court battle, his former owner's sons purchased his freedom and that of his wife in early 1858. Scott worked as a porter in St. Louis, where he died later that year on September 17. Dred Scott died a free man. He is buried in the Calvary Cemetery in St. Louis, Missouri.

nation. In short, one effect of the *Scott* ruling was a stronger, more competitive Republican Party. The decision further hurt the Democrats, who still did not know when to apply the principle of popular sovereignty—at the time of territorial organization or when applying for statehood. Finally, the ruling hurt the image of Court, which lost some of its standing over its interference into the arena of political issues.

## JOHN BROWN'S RAID ON HARPERS FERRY

The United States in 1859 was a divided nation. Slavery continued to be the dominant issue. Unfortunately, slavery was also the one issue on which the North and South could not agree. A radical Northerner took it upon himself to make sure the issue was not forgotten. His name was John Brown. Black abolitionist Frederick Douglass admired Brown. Historian Stephen B. Oates includes Douglass's description of Brown. After meeting the abolitionist, Douglass said, "Brown, though a white gentleman, was in sympathy a black man and as deeply interested in our cause as though his own soul had been pierced with the iron of slavery." Indeed, Brown was intent to destroy slavery. In order to accomplish his goal, Brown embarked upon an outrageous mission in which he hoped to spark a widespread slave rebellion.

Brown received financial backing from six wealthy, influential Northern abolitionists, later called the Secret Six. It is unclear how much these men knew about Brown's plans prior to the raid. Following the raid, in order to avoid possible prosecution, three of the men fled to Canada, another remained in Europe, and one committed himself to an insane asylum. Only one of the six ever admitted to having supported Brown. What is known is that Brown raised the funding necessary to finance his raid.

Brown intended to launch his rebellion by attacking the federal arsenal in Harpers Ferry, Virginia. The arsenal included an armory, which held some 100,000 firearms, more than enough to arm slaves for the pending rebellion. The white abolitionist attempted to enlist Frederick Douglass in his effort. Douglass believed the plan was foolhardy and refused to participate. Brown carried out his plans, anyway. Brown and his assembled raiders waited in a farmhouse located just a few miles away from Harpers Ferry. Despite his best efforts, Brown only had 21 men to accompany him in his plot.

During the evening hours of October 16, 1859, Brown led his band of 21 men toward the federal arsenal at Harpers Ferry. The group was made up of 16 whites and 5 blacks. They moved stealthily into place. At first, everything went as planned. The raiders cut the telegraph lines to prevent anyone from sounding the alarm. Then, they overpowered the single guard and seized the armory and arsenal. Next, Brown and his men collected hostages from Harpers Ferry.

Then, things began to go badly. A baggage master tried to warn an approaching train about the danger. The raiders ordered the man to stop. When the man continued, the raiders fired on him, killing him. The first casualty of the raid, which was intended to start a slave rebellion, was a free black. Strangely, Brown then allowed the train to leave. Word of Brown's raid reached Washington by late morning. Members of the local militia, as well as residents, took up arms against Brown and his men. Instead of starting a rebellion, Brown had provoked the locals into fighting against him. Around noon, the local militia rushed into town and seized control of the bridge. Brown's only escape route was now blocked. The rest of the day consisted of the raiders and locals exchanging small arms fire.

Increasingly coming under fire, casualties for the raiders began to mount. Eight of Brown's men were either dead or dying. Two others had escaped across the river. Facing mounting odds, Brown ordered his raiders into the local firehouse, a small brick building that offered the best chance of defense. During the night, Lieutenant Colonel Robert E. Lee led a unit of Marines to the arsenal. The Marines surrounded the trapped men. Under a white flag, J.E.B. Stuart, then a young lieutenant, approached the engine house. Stuart gave the raiders a note, informing them that if they surrendered, their lives would be spared. Brown rejected the offer, and the Marines stormed the brick building, breaking down the door. They poured in and took Brown, wounded and beaten unconscious, as a prisoner.

Less than 36 hours after Brown's band began the raid, it was over. Brown had failed to free any slaves, and he had failed to start a slave revolt. Instead, 10 of his men were dead, including two of his sons. Brown himself was one of five raiders captured. His captors took him and the others to Charlestown, Virginia. The Commonwealth of Virginia wasted no time in bringing Brown to trial. The abolitionist faced charges of treason, murder, and inciting slaves to rebellion. Brown made use of the public stage, speaking against the evils of slavery. His comments, determination, and conduct during the trial caused many Northerners to reexamine abolitionism and slavery.

On November 2, after deliberating just 45 minutes, the jury returned with three guilty verdicts. Before sentencing, Brown addressed the court. James McPherson quotes part of his speech made that day:

> Now, if it be deemed necessary that I should forfeit my life for the furtherance of the ends of justice, and mingle my blood further with the blood of my children, and with the blood of millions in this slave country whose rights are disregarded by wicked, cruel, and unjust enactments, I submit: so let it be done.

The court handed down a sentence of death, to be carried out a month later. John Brown faced the gallows for his crimes.

Virginia governor Henry Wise feared a rescue attempt. Thus, authorities restricted attendance and access to the execution. Governor Wise ordered some 1,500 soldiers to Charlestown. Few civilians were allowed to attend the hanging. Officials banned Northerners and most journalists from attending the event. Even the soldiers in attendance were kept a distance away from the gallows, out of hearing distance.

On the morning of December 2, 1859, Brown's guard came to his cell. It was time to carry out the sentence of execution. Brown took his silver watch and gave it to his guard as a gesture of thanks for his kind treatment. He also gave him a note, which included his final words. McPherson recalls part of the note's text, which read, "I John Brown am now quite certain that the crimes of this guilty land will never be purged away, but with Blood." The guard escorted Brown out to a wagon, which would carry him to his fate. In the back of the wagon was Brown's coffin. He sat on it as a column of soldiers, waiting nearby, assembled and escorted the wagon to the execution site.

The assembled crowd waited in anticipation. The security measures proved overly cautious. This crowd contained no sympathizers, only those eager to see Brown die. Aside from his guard, Brown approached the gallows alone, having refused the

John Brown, a staunch abolitionist who had been involved in an attack against pro-slavers in Kansas, hoped to incite and arm an uprising of slaves in Harpers Ferry, Virginia, but failed from lack of support. Caught, tried, and sentenced to death, Brown's execution made him a martyr and ominously foreshadowed the upcoming violence of the Civil War. Above, a painting of John Brown kissing a black child on his way to the gallows.

company of any minister who did not condemn slavery. The condemned man bravely and calmly walked up the platform to meet his fate. Several witnesses could not help but admire Brown's courage. His guard placed the noose around Brown's neck, before covering his head with a white linen hood. Then, at the appropriate time, the executioner cut a rope, releasing the platform on which the sentenced man stood. Brown fell through the opening with a thud. The rope held the man for several minutes as the noose choked the life out of him. Soon, John Brown hung lifeless from the end of the rope. The execution was complete.

Southerners rejoiced at the execution of Brown, but church bells all over the North tolled in mourning. American author Henry David Thoreau declared, "This morning Captain Brown was hung. He is not Old Brown any longer; he is an angel of light." While the South viewed Brown as a lunatic, traitor, terrorist, and a danger to society, the North viewed him as someone who died for his beliefs, a victim, and a martyr.

Though he had refused to join the raid on Harpers Ferry, Frederick Douglass was amazed at Brown's commitment to the cause. The former slave also recognized that Brown's efforts led to the Civil War, which resulted in the end of slavery. As quoted on the PBS Web site *Africans in America*, Douglass said, "Did John Brown fail? John Brown began the war that ended American slavery and made this a free Republic. His zeal in the cause of my race was far greater than mine. I could live for the slave, but he could die for him." Indeed, what made John Brown so effective was that what he failed to accomplish in his life, he managed to do with his death. The war against slavery that he wanted to start with the raid on Harpers Ferry was fast approaching.

# The Republican
# Party and
# Abraham Lincoln

In the first half of the decade following the Compromise of 1850, the Whig Party began to unravel. The compromise itself revealed divisions within the party over slavery in the territories. In 1852, the Whigs lost Henry Clay and Daniel Webster when the two leading party figures and dominant statesmen died just four months apart. The party did not have others with the stature and experience of Webster and Clay to lead them. The same year, antislavery Whigs prevented sitting president Millard Fillmore from becoming the Whig presidential nominee. Instead, the Whigs chose Winfield Scott, who managed to win only four states in a loss to Democrat Franklin Pierce. In 1856, the Whigs could not pretend to be a national party and did not even nominate their own candidate, but instead endorsed Millard Fillmore on the Know Nothing Party ticket.

Many Northern Whigs could not bear to associate with those supporting the Kansas-Nebraska Act. In essence, the opening of the western territories to slavery crossed the line of morality for many of these Whigs. Large numbers of Northern

Whigs were disgusted by the stand of their party. Rather than remain linked with pro-slavery men, many Northern Whigs left the party. Some joined the Know Nothing Party, while others left politics altogether. In the South, the slavery issue united politicians above all other issues. As their national party began to splinter, Southern Whigs often switched their party membership and allegiance to the Democrats.

Opponents of the Kansas-Nebraska Act of 1854 began calling themselves Anti-Nebraska Democrats and Anti-Nebraska Whigs. In the coming months and years, many of these individuals found a home in a new party, called the Republicans.

## THE ELECTION OF 1852

In 1852, the Whig Party nominated its last competitive presidential candidate. Winfield Scott ran atop the Whig ticket. Because the former general was a hero of the Mexican-American War, the Whigs hoped Scott would calm Southern fears of Northern antislavery interests. The Democrats nominated Franklin Pierce, who at the time of his inauguration was the youngest man (49 years old) to serve as president. Pierce desired to maintain unity within his party and within the nation, and hoped to avoid issues that split the nation. Events and members of his own party, however, helped catapult those sectional issues to the forefront during his presidency.

There are at least two major reasons why regional issues surfaced during the Pierce presidency. First, several articulate and persuasive antislavery leaders won seats in the House and Senate in the 1850 elections, in part as a reaction against the Compromise of 1850. These men included the likes of Joshua R. Giddings of Ohio and Charles Sumner of Massachusetts. They joined men such as William H. Seward (elected to the Senate in 1849). These men were all fierce foes of slavery, and they used their national office to denounce the South and its peculiar institution.

Formed in 1834, the Whig Party propelled two members into the presidency. The party's demise occurred because members could not agree on issues regarding slavery. Southern Whigs switched allegiances to the Democrat Party while some Northern Whigs created a new group called the Republicans. Above, General Winfield Scott, the last presidential nominee of the Whig Party only won four states against Democrat Franklin Pierce in the 1856 election.

Second, abolitionist and antislavery forces increased their efforts to oppose the Compromise of 1850. This opposition was especially clear in efforts to undermine the Fugitive Slave Act.

Throughout the North, mobs stepped in with attempts to prevent enforcement of this controversial law. Several Northern states also passed new laws protecting personal liberty. Under such laws, state officials could offer some protection to alleged fugitive slaves against bounty hunters and federal commissioners enforcing the Fugitive Slave Act. Some states required a judicial hearing before a resident could be removed from state borders.

The South did not fail to see these actions taken against the Fugitive Slave Act. Such attempts distressed Southerners who believed the Fugitive Slave Act was the one beneficial part of the 1850 compromise. Northern efforts to reverse the act simply convinced many in the South that the North was filled with abolitionists trying to destroy Southern society. Many south of the Mason-Dixon Line believed they were at risk of losing their way of life.

The Kansas-Nebraska Act significantly altered the political landscape. Southern Whigs supported the act, while their Northern counterparts opposed it. This one issue proved to be the wedge that permanently separated the two sides. The controversial act tore apart the Whig Party. The party collapsed, as many Southern Whigs became Democrats. Meanwhile, many Northern Whigs simply withdrew from politics or looked for another party. The development of the Republican Party in 1854 provided a home for many former Whigs.

## THE REPUBLICANS

In February 1854, a group of former Whigs, antislavery Democrats, and Free-Soilers met for a political rally in Ripon, Wisconsin. Those assembled proposed using the name "Republican" to set themselves apart from their old party allegiances. Soon, the Republicans drew support from others opposed to the extension of slavery in the territories.

At first, the Republicans were not a national party. Instead, the new party was entirely limited to the North and West. It quickly established itself as a force in U.S. politics, however. Teaming with the Know Nothing Party, which also opposed the Kansas-Nebraska Act, the Republicans gained control of several state governments in the North and won a majority in the U.S. House of Representatives in the 1854 elections.

## THE ELECTION OF 1856

In 1856, the Republicans held their first nominating convention in Philadelphia. There, the delegates chose John C. Frémont as their candidate for president. Frémont was a former scout and explorer who had traveled extensively out West. Frémont first gained national attention when he participated in the California Bear Flag Revolt during the war with Mexico. The Republicans decided to go with the politically inexperienced adventurer in order to appeal to Democrats and other Northerners who might be looking for a new political home. The Republicans cleverly advertised their platform and candidate with the slogan "Free Soil, Free Labor, Free Men, Frémont." Opponents called them "Black Republicans" due to their political stand against the expansion of slavery.

The election returns revealed the strength of the Republicans in the North. Frémont won 11 Northern states, while Buchanan carried the Deep and Upper South, along with 5 Northern states. Frémont won 114 electoral votes, while Buchanan won the election with 174. Despite the loss, the signs for the Republicans were encouraging. Had Frémont won Pennsylvania and any one of the other Northern states that went to Buchanan—Illinois, Indiana, or New Jersey—then the first Republican presidential candidate would have become the first Republican president. The returns showed that a candidate could win the presidency solely with Northern electoral votes. For many in the South, the election of 1856 served as a warning to the future political strength of their section in national elections. Following Frémont's strong showing in the North, many former Whigs decided the Republican Party was the means to regaining

# The Free Soil Party

The Free Soil Party was a third party that only existed for about six years. In 1848, internal disputes within the Democrat Party led to the formation of the Free Soil Party. Former president Martin Van Buren ran as the Free Soil candidate, likely costing Democrat Lewis Cass the election to the victorious Whig Zachary Taylor. The Free Soil Party membership came from former Whigs and Democrats who opposed slavery. The party opposed the expansion of slavery into the territories, but its members were not abolitionists. Free-Soilers maintained that slavery was economically and morally inferior to free men on free soil. The party wanted to open up western lands to free men, supporting a homestead act that would give land to settlers.

The party platform supported "Free Soil, Free Speech, Free Labor, and Free Men." After failing to win more than 5 percent of the vote in the 1852 election, the party began to collapse. Many Free Soil members ended up joining the Republican Party after its founding in 1854. Although short-lived, the Free Soil Party left its mark on the U.S. political system: Many of the ideas that this third party advocated later became the core of the Republicans, which remains one of the two parties in the traditional two-party system today.

political power. During the next four years, the Republican Party began to broaden its platform in order to build a stronger, more attractive party.

## THE LINCOLN-DOUGLAS DEBATES

The 1858 Senate election in the state of Illinois drew national attention. At that time, state legislatures chose senators. Thus, U.S. Senate candidates campaigned for members of their party in an effort to win a majority in the state legislature. In 1858, the two candidates for the Illinois Senate seat symbolized their respective parties, especially in their approach to slavery. Stephen A. Douglas was one of the North's most well-known Democrats. Douglas championed the idea of popular sovereignty to decide the issue of slavery. Douglas, however, faced opposition from his own party establishment for his principled stand against the Lecompton constitution, citing his conviction that residents of a territory or state ought to decide the issue for themselves. President Buchanan backed several Democrat candidates against Douglas.

On the Republican side was Abraham Lincoln, who had been a leading member of the Whig Party in Illinois. He had served a single term in the U.S. House of Representatives. During his time in Congress, Lincoln had distinguished himself by opposing James K. Polk, demanding the president show the "spot" on U.S. soil that Mexicans had shed American blood. Lincoln's disagreement with the Mexican-American War resulted in protests in his district. Facing almost certain defeat in the next election, Lincoln decided to return to practicing law in Springfield, Illinois. In 1858, Lincoln was the most important Republican figure in Illinois. His senate campaign that year launched him onto the national stage, making him a leading candidate for the Republican presidential nomination in 1860.

Lincoln and Douglas agreed to a series of seven debates, held throughout the state over a period of two months. The debates helped each candidate define himself. More importantly, the debates helped the Republicans define themselves as a national party. Lincoln opposed slavery, but he was no abolitionist. The debates demonstrated Lincoln's moderation on the slavery issue, although many in the South still believed him and all other Republicans to be abolitionists.

Perhaps the most significant debate occurred at Freeport, Illinois. There, Lincoln asked Douglas to explain his support for popular sovereignty in the territories. Since the Supreme Court

*The Lincoln-Douglas debates showcased two of the most prolific politicians of the Civil War era: Senator Stephen Douglas and newcomer Abraham Lincoln. Douglas, a Northern Democrat who developed popular sovereignty, did not support or condemn slavery; Lincoln, on the other hand, wished to limit slavery's spread to new territories. The popular debates, held in seven locations throughout Illinois, catapulted Lincoln into national politics. Above, Lincoln addresses the public during one of the debates.*

ruled slavery restrictions to be unconstitutional in the *Dred Scott* case, Lincoln wanted to know if Douglas believed local citizens could still restrict slavery by exercising their popular sovereignty. Douglas remained consistent to his convictions, answering that the legal status of slavery (legal or illegal) depended upon the support of local authorities. In other words, popular sovereignty still decided the issue of slavery, in the territories, in the states, anywhere. Despite the *Dred Scott* ruling, a territory could prohibit slavery by the laws it passed or failed to pass. Douglas's response outraged the South. His answer became known as the Freeport Doctrine or Freeport Heresy.

In the end, Lincoln proved to be a capable opponent and excellent candidate. At the time, as required by the Constitution, senators were chosen by their state legislatures, not by popular election. Thus, Lincoln and Douglas actually campaigned for members of their respective parties for seats in the Illinois legislature. The Republicans received more votes than the Democrats, but the Democrat-controlled legislature had manipulated the districts to favor their party. Thus, Douglas won the Senate seat, even though Lincoln's party won more votes.

Lincoln's run for the Senate propelled him to the national stage. He was no longer an unknown, a former one-term congressman from Illinois. Instead, he was a well known spokesman for the Republican Party—and he was also a leading candidate for the Republican nomination for president in 1860.

## THE ELECTION OF 1860

The 1860 presidential race was one of the most conflicted elections in U.S. history. The issue of slavery, which had been simmering beneath the surface for many years, was now the main issue. No longer did any of the parties pretend to ignore slavery. Indeed, the Republican Party was created as a response to the slavery issue. In the year prior to the election, John Brown had embarked on his radical and unsuccessful attempt to start a slave rebellion by leading a raid on Harpers Ferry, Virginia. His execution further divided the nation over the issue and morality of slavery. The South feared the North was filled with radical abolitionists seeking to destroy the Southern way of life. At the same time, many in the North believed Southerners were bent on extending slavery everywhere, even into the free states of the North. The nation was already showing signs of being torn apart by slavery. The two-party system collapsed, splintering into four major candidates, each with support from different sections of the country.

The Democrats met in April to choose their candidate. Party leaders had chosen Charleston as the site for their convention in an attempt to soothe Southern fears over Stephen Douglas of Illinois, the likely nominee. The tactic backfired when Southern delegates walked out of the convention after losing a vote to include a federal slave code for the western territories in the party platform. Western delegates argued instead for popular sovereignty. Unable to unite, the Democrats adjourned their convention without choosing a candidate. Northern Democrats later met in Baltimore, where they selected Stephen Douglas as their nominee. The Baltimore convention also ratified their support of popular sovereignty to deal with slavery in the territories. Southern Democrats met in Richmond, nominating John C. Breckenridge, Buchanan's vice president, as their candidate. The Southern convention passed a resolution supporting the protection of slavery rights in the territories. The Democrats presented a divided front.

In contrast, the Republicans emerged from their convention united behind a single candidate and a well-defined and attractive platform. The Republicans clearly stated their opposition to the expansion of slavery. Heading into the convention, William H. Seward was the likely nominee. Seward's ties with elements of the radical antislavery movement hurt his chances, however.

Party leaders recognized the need to be something more than merely an antislavery party. The platform included an aggressive economic policy, including a homestead bill, assistance for a transcontinental railroad, and internal improvements funded by the federal government. The platform also included a prohibition of slavery in the territories. To assure states in both the South and the North, the platform also contained provisions guaranteeing states the power to decide the legality of slavery within their own borders.

To represent their bold platform, the Republicans chose Abraham Lincoln of Springfield, Illinois. Lincoln was an ideal candidate for several reasons. He was from a western state, enabling him to challenge Douglas. The tall, lanky Lincoln was also a gifted speaker. More importantly, among well-known Republicans, he was the most moderate on the issue of slavery. As the election approached, however, Southern radicals vowed to secede if Lincoln won the election.

Finally, the newly formed Constitutional Union Party presented Tennessee senator John Bell as its candidate for president. Former conservative Whigs who wanted to preserve the Union established the party with former Know Nothings who did not support the Republicans. As the name of the party suggests, the platform had one primary goal: maintaining the unity of the Union by recognizing only the authority of the Constitution. Their clear-cut platform stated their commitment "to recognize no political principle other than the Constitution of the Country, the Union of the States, and the Enforcement of the Laws." The party attempted to sidestep the issue of slavery by not taking a stand on it. Bell managed to win three states in the election: Tennessee, Kentucky, and Virginia. The party lasted only for the 1860 election.

In many respects, the election was a tale of two different contests. In the North, Lincoln and Douglas competed against each other, with Breckenridge and Bell battling each other in the South. Lincoln's support was confined to the North and West, while the Deep South backed Breckenridge. Douglas won Missouri and part of New Jersey and Bell carried three states in the Upper South. Lincoln won 17 free states, while Breckenridge carried 11 slave states. Douglas won nearly 30 percent of the popular vote, but only 12 electoral votes, coming in fourth in the Electoral College. Breckenridge received 72 electoral votes, while Bell claimed 39. Lincoln and the Republicans were essentially a regional party, their support limited to the North. Lincoln's name did not even appear on the ballot in the

Southern states. He received fewer than 40 percent of the popular vote. Nevertheless, the man from Illinois won 180 electoral votes, giving him a majority and winning him the presidency. The Republicans had elected their first president.

The election of Lincoln served to speed Southern secession. Within weeks of Lincoln's election, South Carolina began considering withdrawing from the Union. On December 20, 1860, it did so. The United States was certainly not united anymore. Moreover, Abraham Lincoln would not take office until March 4, 1861. Between these two dates, the stage was set for war between the two sections.

# Secession and the Coming War

Abraham Lincoln's election shook the South. Militants demanded the South secede from the Union. These separatists, called "Fire-Eaters" by Northerners, agitated for secession. To advance their radical doctrine, the Fire-Eaters convinced many in the South that Lincoln and the Republicans intended to abolish slavery. Rather than submit to Northern tyranny, secessionists argued that Southern states should leave the Union and form their own nation, one that guaranteed the right to own slaves.

## BUCHANAN'S FAILURE

As the secession crisis loomed, outgoing president James Buchanan did little to help the situation. Buchanan insisted secession was unconstitutional, but also believed he lacked any constitutional authority to prevent it. Thus, President Buchanan refused to take action as states left the Union and built up their defenses, often at the expense of the U.S. military.

Senator John J. Crittenden of Kentucky offered a proposal in an attempt to avert the crisis. The so-called Crittenden Compromise proposed a series of amendments to the Constitution. Crittenden hoped these amendments would appease the South. The amendments were to guarantee the legality of slavery in Southern states, while another guaranteed fugitive-slave law enforcement. The key part of the Crittenden Compromise,

## The Politics of Secession

After Lincoln won the 1860 election, states in the Deep South began to secede. States in the Upper South, however, such as Virginia, at first adopted a wait-and-see approach to the situation. The Commonwealth of Virginia seceded from the Union on April 17, 1861, but there were many within the state who did not want to leave the Union. This was especially true for the western counties of Virginia. The terrain was mountainous and very few of the residents there owned slaves.

The Virginia voting public overwhelmingly voted in favor of secession on May 23, ratifying actions the legislature had taken a month earlier. The western counties of Virginia strongly opposed secession, voting 2 to 1 to stay in the Union. These same counties cast more than half the votes against secession in the referendum. Virginia, however, had already left the Union and joined the Confederacy.

The western counties of Virginia then took steps to secede from Virginia. These counties elected representatives who met in Wheeling and established a government. The western counties elected their own governor and legislature and even sent their senators to Washington. This government claimed to be the legitimate governing authority over the state of Virginia. In October 1861, in an however, was the re-establishment of the 36° 30' line of the Missouri Compromise. Crittenden proposed that the 36° 30' line be extended in all U.S. territory currently held or acquired in the future. In other words, slavery would be allowed south of the line and prohibited north of it.

Understandably, representatives from the border states were supportive of the plan, which received mixed reactions

election with very low turnout, the western counties voted to form their own state. (Many later argued that the presence of Union troops prevented those favoring secession to vote.) At first, officials were going to name this state Kanawha, after one of the counties. The convention later decided to call the new state West Virginia.

A convention to draw up a constitution was held later in the year. The convention included some strange situations, including an instance in which a delegate lived in one district, but represented another. This convention produced a constitution and asked Congress and the president to admit West Virginia as a new state. Congress approved, and Lincoln endorsed the application on December 31, 1862, but the president added one requirement: The constitution had to provide for the gradual abolition of slavery. The state convention met again and inserted the necessary wording. In late March 1862, West Virginia ratified its revised constitution. On April 20, President Abraham Lincoln issued a proclamation admitting West Virginia into the Union, effective on June 20, 1863. West Virginia was now a state.

Following the war, the Commonwealth of Virginia sued to reclaim West Virginia on the grounds that secession was unconstitutional. This was ironic, considering that West Virginia seceded from Virginia after Virginia had seceded from the Union. The U.S. Supreme Court ruled in 1870 that West Virginia had followed each of the steps necessary to become a state as outlined in the Constitution. Therefore, the Court determined that the admission of West Virginia into the Union was constitutional.

from the rest of the states. Apparently, Southern senators offered to support the compromise if Republicans would also agree to support it. This was a bold request, considering the Republican Party was founded upon the idea that slavery should not be allowed to expand. After the election and before the president-elect took office, Republican leaders met privately with Lincoln, still in Springfield, Illinois, and decided to reject the compromise.

Just six weeks after Lincoln's election, on December 20, 1860, South Carolina seceded from the Union. In January, Mississippi, Florida, Alabama, Georgia, and Louisiana also seceded, followed by Texas on February 1. The seven states then took steps to form a new government and elected their leaders. Jefferson Davis took the oath of office as president of the Confederate States of America on February 18, 1861, two weeks before Lincoln's inauguration. The ceremony took place on the steps of the Alabama state Capitol in Montgomery, Alabama. One week after Lincoln was sworn in, on March 11, the Confederate States of America adopted its constitution. The C.S.A. Constitution was essentially the same as the U.S. Constitution, though it notably guaranteed the right to own slaves and denied the Confederate Congress the power to limit slavery in states or territories.

## PRESIDENT LINCOLN

On March 4, 1861, Abraham Lincoln took the oath of office, becoming the sixteenth president of the United States. He faced the most daunting constitutional crisis in the nation's history. In his inaugural address (which can be found at the Avalon Project Web site), Lincoln tried to reassure Southerners of his intentions, saying, "I have no purpose, directly or indirectly, to interfere with the institution of slavery in the States where it exists. I believe I have no lawful right to do so, and I have no inclination to do so."

Lincoln also expressed his conviction that "the central idea of secession is the essence of anarchy," or chaos and rebellion. The new president believed that since the South was in the minority within a system that made decisions by majority vote, then the South would likely lose some of the political battles. Because seceding states had rejected the rule of the majority, they were choosing anarchy, or chaos, instead. Lincoln opposed secession, insisting that "no State upon its own mere motion can lawfully get out of the Union." To Lincoln, secession violated the Constitution.

Lincoln also summarized the whole issue underlying secession, saying, "One section of our country believes slavery is right and ought to be extended, while the other believes it is wrong and ought not to be extended. This is the only substantial dispute." To Lincoln, and indeed, to most Americans in 1861, the secession crisis was not about states' rights, territories, or election results. Instead, the crisis facing the United States had slavery as its roots. Generally, the South wanted to expand slavery within the growing nation, and the North wanted to limit slavery to the Southern states where it already existed.

Finally, Lincoln promised to do what he could to hold the Union together. Because several states had already seceded, Lincoln stated that, as president, he intended to protect federal property, wherever it might be. "The power confided to me," he declared, "will be used to hold, occupy, and possess the property and places belonging to the Government." Lincoln had no intentions of turning over Fort Sumter or Fort Pickens, both located in the South, to the Confederacy.

Lincoln, however, soon learned he had little time to wait. On the day of his inauguration, the new president went to his office and received a disturbing message from the commander of one of the two remaining federal forts in Southern territory. Fort Sumter had only enough supplies to hold out about six weeks. Unless the forces there received the necessary supplies,

*When Abraham Lincoln was elected president in 1860, many Southerners believed it was the beginning of the end of slavery. Despite the best efforts of a few politicians, South Carolina was the first to secede the Union, followed shortly by six other states. At the same time Lincoln was being sworn into office during his inauguration (above), the newly formed Confederate States of America were creating their own government and constitution.*

Lincoln would be forced to evacuate the fort. The new president was unwilling to abandon the fort, especially since he had just promised to protect all federal property.

## THE APPROACHING CRISIS

When Lincoln took office, there were only two federal military forts in the South still held by Union forces. These two forts were both located on the coast: Fort Pickens in Florida and Fort Sumter in South Carolina. Fort Pickens lay near Pensacola, Florida, and enjoyed an isolated position outside the Pensacola Harbor. Fort Sumter was one of four federal military properties in Charleston, South Carolina. The other three were Castle Pinckney, Fort Johnson, and Fort Moultrie. Sumter was unique, because it was located on a small island in the entrance to the harbor. The others, situated on land, were therefore exposed to danger from land forces. Although Fort Sumter lay in the harbor, its nearness to the other forts and Charleston itself meant that enemy forces on the land could bombard it from three sides. Defensive positions on land were capable of easily denying relief ships from reaching Fort Sumter.

South Carolinians resented the federal troops stationed on what they believed to be the soil of an independent state. Tensions rose even higher when South Carolina seceded on December 20, 1860. Because Congress did not recognize South Carolina as independent, the federal troops remained in Fort Moultrie. Their commanding officer, however, Major Robert Anderson, recognized their vulnerable position. Hoping to delay a possible attack, Anderson secretly moved his 85 men under the cover of darkness on December 26 from Fort Moultrie to the more defensible Fort Sumter in the harbor. The move was both bold and necessary. Lincoln had not ordered Anderson to relocate, but the situation demanded it. South Carolinians condemned the move, but did nothing other than occupy the forts on land and demand Anderson to evacuate completely from South Carolina soil. When other states seceded, forming the Confederate States of America, Confederate General Pierre G.T. Beauregard insisted that Anderson and his men withdraw.

Anderson refused to budge, however, and awaited further orders from Washington. The fort itself was unfinished and undersupplied. During the Buchanan presidency, cuts in military spending meant the forces inside the fort had less than half the number of cannons they required. Worse still, Anderson had dwindling rations. For the federal troops inside Fort Sumter, there was little to do but wait for orders to leave, or await an attack from shore.

Buchanan ordered the fort re-supplied, sending the steamer *Star of the West* to deliver troops and supplies. When the relief ship arrived on January 9, 1861, however, Southern artillery opened fire, forcing the ship to withdraw and return north. According to historian Brian Holden Reid, "Buchanan believed that, although secession was illegal, the federal government had no power to resist it." Holden Reid describes Buchanan's strategy for the last four months of his presidency as nothing more than to "leave office without provoking war." This explains the ill-fated attempt to deliver supplies by *Star of the West*, which turned back after coming under enemy fire. Buchanan's half-hearted attempt to re-supply Fort Sumter only served to anger the South and draw attention to the continued presence of federal troops in the Charleston Harbor. Anderson had only enough supplies to remain in the fort until April 15.

Lincoln was placed in an awkward political situation, and decided to order a fleet of ships to deliver supplies to Fort Sumter. It was a difficult decision, for if the new president acted too boldly and war broke out, then blame would likely fall on him. On the other hand, if Lincoln simply surrendered the fort, then he would be guilty of breaking his pledge to "hold, occupy, and possess" all federal property within the seceded states. In a move that foreshadowed many Lincoln decisions, the new president sidestepped the issue and forced the Confederate government to make an equally distasteful choice.

Confederate representatives went to Washington, offering to negotiate a peace treaty and to purchase federal properties within their borders. Lincoln refused to meet with any Confederate negotiators, arguing the Confederate States of America was not a legitimate government. Any negotiations with Confederate officials would effectively recognize the Confederacy as an independent and lawful government. Secretary of State William Seward secretly met with Confederate agents in an attempt to secure some sort of peace deal. The efforts failed, however, and Seward loyally backed Lincoln throughout the war.

On the other side, the Confederate government, which formed in early February, faced some difficult decisions as to how to deal with Fort Sumter. The first major issue was the question of authority. That is, should the Confederate government or South Carolina decide whether to negotiate or attack? South Carolina officials believed the fort belonged to their state. Confederate president Jefferson Davis, however, did not want the South to be viewed as the attacker in the situation. Davis and Lincoln both understood that the border states had not yet decided their course. Any unnecessary aggression might result in those states siding with the other side.

Ultimately, Confederate officials determined the issue was one that affected the new nation and decided to take control of the forces in Charleston. Jefferson Davis sent General Beauregard to take command of the forces in South Carolina. Beauregard, overseeing the siege of Fort Sumter, called on Anderson to surrender or evacuate the fort. Anderson refused, and Beauregard cut off all food supplies from the city to the fort. Throughout March, the two sides waited. While they waited, they prepared for the coming fight.

On April 4, President Lincoln determined that he had to send relief to Fort Sumter or the garrison would be forced to withdraw for lack of supplies. The president sent a group of civilian ships, escorted by naval ships, to Charleston. Then, on April 6, Lincoln took an extraordinary step. Lincoln informed the South Carolina governor that he only intended to send supplies, not reinforcements, into the fort. As long as Southern authorities did not attack or stop the supply ships, Lincoln promised to send no troops or weapons to the fort.

Now Jefferson Davis and his government faced a difficult situation. If Northern ships reached the harbor, then Confederate forces would need to repel their attempts to re-supply the fort. If Union ships managed to reach the fort, then Anderson and his garrison could continue to hold out. If the federal forces simply abandoned the fort, the chance to drive them out of a Southern-claimed possession would be lost. Many troops wanted to attack the fort. Secretary of State of the Confederacy Robert Toombs argued against the attack, believing it would lead to Northern support against the South. Speaking of the attack, author Robert N. Rosen records that Toombs reportedly stated, "It is unnecessary. It puts us in the wrong. It is fatal." After heated debate, Davis overruled Toombs and decided on April 9 to give Beauregard permission to attack the fort in order to force its surrender.

Beauregard sent representatives to the fort under a flag of truce on April 11 to deliver an ultimatum. During this meeting, Major Anderson reportedly informed Beauregard and the Confederates of his shaky situation. According to the National Park Service, Anderson stated, "Gentlemen, if you do not batter the fort to pieces about us, we shall be starved out in a few days." This should have been welcome news to the Confederates. Instead, the report spurred them into action. Beauregard knew that the relief ships were approaching and were expected to arrive before April 15. The Confederate general decided not to wait for Anderson to leave, but rather to drive him from the fort.

## FORT SUMTER

Inside the fort, Major Anderson and his men waited for the attack they were certain was coming. After midnight on April 12,

*Located in South Carolina, Fort Sumter became the site of the first standoff and military battle of the Civil War. After a series of negotiations with the Confederates, Union troops refused to evacuate the stronghold and were subsequently bombarded by artillery fire. One day after the attack, Lincoln called for 75,000 volunteers to quash the rebellion.*

1861, Beauregard tried again to get Anderson to surrender or promise to withdraw. His efforts were unsuccessful. Around 3:20 A.M., Confederate forces informed Anderson that they would begin an artillery attack in one hour. Around 4:30 A.M., a Confederate gun launched a single mortar shot over Fort Sumter. The first bombardment of the war had just begun. Confederate artillery crews fired from Cummings Point, Fort Johnson, and Fort Moultrie.

## The Fort Sumter Flag

After Major Anderson lowered the flag from Fort Sumter, he took it with him when he returned to the North. The flag was presented at rallies and other public gatherings to garner support for the war. On April 20, 1861, Anderson presented the flag at a rally in New York City. More than 100,000 people packed into Union Square as the flag was raised atop a statue of George Washington riding a horse. Officials then took the flag on a tour throughout the North in order to raise money for the war. Officials would offer the flag up for public auction, though it was understood that the purchaser would then donate it back to the Union, allowing organizers to continue using the flag to raise money. Throughout the conflict, the Fort Sumter flag was widely recognized as a patriotic symbol for the Union.

Despite Union attempts to retake Fort Sumter, the Confederates held the harbor fort until the final weeks of the war. After Union forces reclaimed Fort Sumter, Robert Anderson, who had achieved the rank of major general, returned to active duty in order to raise the Fort Sumter flag over the fort on April 14, 1865—exactly four years after he had been forced to lower it. The original Fort Sumter flag is now on display in the Fort Sumter Museum.

Residents of Charleston watched the bombardment. Also there that night was Edmund Ruffin, a celebrated secessionist. Ruffin had traveled to Charleston to be a part of the beginning of the war. Following the signal shot, Ruffin lit the first cannon that fired on the fort.

Inside the fort, Anderson and his guns remained silent for the first two and a half hours of the attack. The fort was designed to wage war on naval ships, which could not fire rounds high into the air. Although Anderson had 60 large guns, he lacked the necessary men to operate them. Anderson also made the decision not to expose his men unnecessarily to enemy fire. Thus, the most effective guns in the fort were not fired, since they were also the most exposed positions.

The artillery barrage lasted throughout April 12 and all through that night. At one point the flagpole, located in the center of the fort complex, fell. While the men inside the fort tried to rig some sort of substitute, the Confederates sent representatives to determine if the lowered flag meant surrender. Union soldiers raised the U.S. flag, but the two sides entered into negotiations. On April 13 at 2:00 P.M., Anderson agreed to surrender Fort Sumter. The official surrender took place the next day when the federal troops withdrew from the fort.

Amazingly, neither side suffered a fatality during the bombardment. Only nine soldiers suffered serious injuries—four Confederates and five Union men. Anderson, however, demanded the right to fire a 100-gun salute to the U.S. flag as part of the withdrawal terms. An accident occurred during this salute, resulting in an explosion that killed one Union soldier and seriously wounded another. Anderson ended the salute after firing 50 rounds. Then, Major Anderson ordered the Fort Sumter flag lowered.

The relief ships that Lincoln had sent now arrived, and Anderson's men clambered aboard to return to the North. Union troops marched out of the fort and boarded the ferries. The Confederates held Charleston Harbor for the remainder of the war.

After the fall of Fort Sumter, President Lincoln sent out a call for 75,000 volunteers to enlist for 90 days in order to put down the rebellion. The South cheered the news, and four other Southern states left the Union within five weeks. The slaveholding states of Virginia, Arkansas, Tennessee, and North Carolina seceded and joined the Confederacy. Missouri, Kentucky, Maryland, and Delaware were the four remaining U.S. states in which slavery was legal. It was almost certain that Delaware intended to stay in the Union, but the fate of the other three border states was in doubt. President Lincoln took steps to make sure these states stayed in the Union. The long, bloody war, which many believed would be short-lived, had finally begun.

# Glossary

**ABOLITION**  The outlawing of slavery in the United States.

**ABOLITIONIST**  A person who wanted to end, or abolish, slavery in the United States.

**CIVIL WAR**  A war between two sides made up of citizens from the same country.

**COMPROMISE**  An agreement in which each side gives up some of its demands and accepts some of the things it did not want in order to reach a conclusion to an argument.

**CONFEDERACY**  The Confederate States of America, formed by the Southern states that seceded from the Union from 1860 to 1861.

**EMANCIPATION**  The act of freeing slaves.

**INAUGURATION**  The swearing-in ceremony in which the new U.S. president officially takes office.

**FIRE-EATER**  A Southerner who was strongly opposed to any restrictions on slavery.

**FREE SOIL**  A territory or state in which slavery was prohibited.

**FREE-SOILER**  A person opposed to the extension of slavery.

**NEUTRAL**  The act of not taking a side during a conflict.

**NULLIFICATION**  The actions of a state government to prevent the enforcement of a federal law within the borders of a state.

**PECULIAR INSTITUTION**  Slavery.

**POPULAR SOVEREIGNTY**  The belief that settlers in a territory had the right to choose, by popular vote, whether or not to allow slavery.

**REBELS**   Northern nickname for the citizens of the states that seceded and joined the Confederacy during the Civil War.

**SECESSION**   The act of seceding from or leaving a nation.

**TARIFF**   Government charge or duty (tax) placed on imported items.

**UNCONSTITUTIONAL**   Describing a legislative act or government action that conflicts with the Constitution, meaning it is in violation of the principles of the Constitution.

**UNION**   The Northern states that remained loyal to the United States during the Civil War.

**YANKEES**   Southern nickname for citizens of the Northern states.

# Bibliography

Abrahamson, James L. *The Men of Secession and Civil War, 1859–1861.* Wilmington, Del.: Scholarly Resources, 2000.

Ayers, Edward L. *What Caused the Civil War? Reflections on the South and Southern History.* New York: W.W. Norton, 2005.

Barney, William H. *Battleground for the Union: The Era of the Civil War and Reconstruction, 1848–1877.* Englewood Cliffs, N.J.: Prentice-Hall, 1990.

Boritt, Gabor S., ed. *Why the Civil War Came.* New York: Oxford University Press, 1996.

Brinkley, Alan, et al. *American History: A Survey.* New York: McGraw-Hill, 1991.

Brock, William R., ed. *The Civil War.* New York: Harper & Row, 1969.

Bryant, William Cullen, II. (comp.) *Power for Sanity: Selected Editorials of William Cullen Bryant, 1829–1861.* New York: Fordham University Press, 1994.

Calore, Paul. *The Causes of the Civil War: The Political, Cultural, Economic, and Territorial Disputes between North and South.* Jefferson, N.C.: McFarland & Company, 2008.

Collins, Bruce. *The Origins of America's Civil War.* New York: Holmes and Meier Publishers, 1981.

Craven, Avery. *The Coming of the Civil War.* Chicago: The University of Chicago Press, 1957.

———. *Civil War in the Making.* Baton Rouge: Louisiana State University Press, 1959.

Cummins, D. Duane, and William Gee White. *The Origins of the Civil War.* Encino, Calif.: Glencoe Publishing, 1979.

Dumond, Dwight Lowell. *Antislavery Origins of the Civil War in the United States.* Ann Arbor: The University of Michigan Press, 1959.

Fehrenbacher, Don E. *The Dred Scott Case: Its Significance in American Law and Politics.* New York: Oxford University Press, 1978.

Formby, John. *The American Civil War: A Concise History of Its Causes, Progress, and Results*. New York: Charles Scribner's Sons, 1910.

Fowler, William Chauncey. *The Sectional Controversy*. New York: Charles Scribner, 1863.

Freehling, William W. *Prelude to Civil War: The Nullification Controversy in South Carolina 1816–1836*. New York: Harper and Row, 1965.

———. *The Road to Disunion: Secessionists at Bay 1776–1854*. Oxford, England: Oxford University Press, 1990.

Goldston, Robert. *The Coming of the Civil War*. New York: The Macmillan Company, 1972.

Grant, Susan-Mary. *The War for a Nation: The American Civil War*. New York: Routledge, 2006.

Hansen, Harry. *The Civil War: A History*. New York: Penguin Books, 1961.

Hart, Albert Bushnell, ed. *Causes of the Civil War: 1859–1861*. The American Nation: A History. Vol. 19. New York: Harper & Brothers Publishers, 1906.

Holden Reid, Brian. *The Origins of the American Civil War*. London: Longman, 1996.

Julius, Kevin C. *The Abolitionist Decade, 1829–1838: A Year by Year History of Early Events in the Antislavery Movement*. Jefferson, N.C.: McFarland & Company, 2004.

Levine, Bruce C. *Half Slave and Half Free: The Roots of Civil War*. New York: Hill and Wang, 1992.

Linden, Glenn M. *Voices from the Gathering Storm: The Coming of the American Civil War*. Wilmington, Del.: Scholarly Resources, 2001.

McPherson, James M. *Battle Cry of Freedom: The Civil War Era*. Oxford, England: Oxford University Press, 1988.

———. *Ordeal by Fire: The Civil War and Reconstruction*. New York: Alfred A. Knopf, 1982.

Niven, John. *The Coming of the Civil War: 1837–1861*. Arlington Heights, Ill.: Harlan Davidson, 1990.

Noll, Mark A. *The Civil War as a Theological Crisis*. Chapel Hill: The University of North Carolina Press, 2006.

Oates, Stephen B. *The Approaching Fury: Voices of the Storm, 1820–1861.* New York: Harper Collins Publishers, 1997.

O'Connor, Thomas H. *The Lords of the Loom: The Cotton Whigs and the Coming of the Civil War.* New York: Charles Scribner's Sons, 1968.

Padover, Saul K. *Jefferson.* Old Saybrook, Conn.: Konecky & Konecky, 1942.

Ravitch, Diane. *The American Reader: Words that Moved a Nation.* New York: HarperCollins, 2000.

Rosen, Robert N. *Confederate Charleston: An Illustrated History of the City and the People During the Civil War.* Columbia: The University of South Carolina Press, 1994.

Rozwenc, Edwin C., ed. *Slavery as a Cause of the Civil War.* Boston: D.C. Heath and Company, 1963.

———. *The Causes of the American Civil War.* Boston: D.C. Heath and Company, 1961.

Schoultz, Lars. *Beneath the United States: A History of U.S. Policy Toward Latin America.* Cambridge, Mass.: Harvard University Press, 1998.

Seidman, Rachel Filene. *The Civil War: A History in Documents.* Oxford, England: Oxford University Press, 2001.

Stampp, Kenneth M., ed. *The Causes of the Civil War.* Englewood Cliffs, N.J.: Prentice-Hall, 1965.

Stuart, Reginald C. *United States Expansionism and British North America, 1775–1871.* Chapel Hill: The University of North Carolina Press, 1988.

Tenzer, Lawrence R. *The Forgotten Cause of the Civil War: A New Look at the Slavery Issue.* Manahawkin, N.J.: Scholars' Publishing House, 1997.

Trefousse, Hans L., ed. *The Causes of the Civil War: Institutional Failure or Human Blunder?* New York: Holt, Rinehart and Winston, 1971.

Walther, Eric H. *The Shattering of the Union: America in the 1850s.* Lanham, Md.: Scholarly Resources, 2004.

Weeks, William Earl. *Building the Continental Empire: American Expansion from the Revolution to the Civil War.* Chicago: Ivan R. Dee, 1996.

Weinberg, Albert K. *Manifest Destiny: A Study of Nationalist Expansionism in American History*. Baltimore: Johns Hopkins University Press, 1935.

Whitridge, Arnold. *No Compromise! The Story of the Fanatics Who Paved the Way to the Civil War*. New York: Farrar, Straus and Cudahy, 1960.

# Further Resources

Arnold, James R., and Roberta Wiener. *Divided in Two: The Road to Civil War, 1861*. Minneapolis: Lerner Publications Company, 2002.

Epperson, James F. *Causes of the Civil War*. Stockton, N.J.: OTTN Publishing, 2005.

Imbriaco, Alison. *Causes of the Civil War*. Berkeley Heights, N.J.: Enslow Publishers, 2004.

Naden, Corinne J., and Rose Blue. *Why Fight? The Causes of the American Civil War*. Austin, Tx.: Raintree Steck-Vaughn Publishers, 2000.

Peacock, Judith. *Secession: The Southern States Leave the Union*. Mankato, Minn.: Bridgestone Books, 2003.

## WEB SITES

Constitution Society: Text of the Webster-Hayne Debate
http://www.constitution.org/hwdebate/webstr2d.htm

Fort Sumter National Monument
http://www.nps.gov/history/history/online_books/hh/12/hh12f.htm

John Brown's Holy War
http://www.pbs.org/wgbh/amex/brown/filmmore/transcript/transcript1.html

Library of Congress: Transcript of a Letter from Thomas Jefferson to John Holmes
http://www.loc.gov/exhibits/jefferson/159.html

Lincoln's First Inaugural Address
http://avalon.law.yale.edu/19th_century/lincoln1.asp

Lincoln's "House Divided" Speech
http://www.pbs.org/wgbh/aia/part4/4h2934t.html

Northwest Ordinance, July 13, 1787
http://avalon.law.yale.edu/18th_century/nworder.asp

U.S. Supreme Court Center: *Scott v. Sandford*
http://supreme.justia.com/us/60/393/case.html

# Picture Credits

# Index

# About
# the Authors

---

**DR. SHANE MOUNTJOY**  resides in York, Nebraska, where he is associate professor of history and dean of students at York College. Recognized by his peers and students as an outstanding teacher, Professor Mountjoy insists he is still just a student at heart. He has earned degrees from York College, Lubbock Christian University, the University of Nebraska, and the University of Missouri. He and his wife home school their four daughters, Macy, Karlie, Ainsley, and Tessa. He is the author of several books, including *Technology and the Civil War*, also in THE CIVIL WAR: A NATION DIVIDED series.

**TIM MCNEESE** is associate professor of history at York College in York, Nebraska, where he is in his seventeenth year of college instruction. Professor McNeese earned an associate of arts degree from York College, a bachelor of arts in history and political science from Harding University, and a master of arts in history from Missouri State University. A prolific author of books for elementary, middle and high school, and college readers, McNeese has published more than 100 books and educational materials over the past 20 years, on everything from the founding of early New York to Hispanic authors. His writing has earned him a citation in the library reference work *Contemporary Authors*, and multiple citations in *Best Books for Young Teen Readers*. In 2006, McNeese appeared on the History Channel program *Risk Takers, History Makers: John Wesley Powell and the Grand Canyon*. He was a faculty member at the 2006 Tony Hillerman Writers Conference in Albuquerque. His wife, Beverly, is an assistant professor of English at York College. They have two married children, Noah and Summer, and three grandchildren, Ethan, Adrianna, and Finn William. Tim and Bev McNeese sponsored study trips for college students on the Lewis and Clark Trail in 2003 and 2005 and to the American Southwest in 2008. You may contact Professor McNeese at tdmcneese@york.edu.